THE VISION OF THE BELOVED DISCIPLE

THE VISION OF THE BELOVED DISCIPLE
Meeting Jesus in the Gospel of John

George T. Montague, SM

ALBA·HOUSE   **alba house**   NEW·YORK

SOCIETY OF ST. PAUL, 2187 VICTORY BLVD., STATEN ISLAND, NEW YORK 10314

ST PAULS

Library of Congress Cataloging-in-Publication Data

Montague, George T.
    The vision of the beloved disciple : meeting Jesus in the Gospel of John /
    George T. Montague.
        p. cm.
    ISBN 0-8189-0835-1
    1. Bible. N.T. John—Criticism, interpreation, etc.   I. Title.

    BS2615.2. M585 2000
    226.5'06—dc21

                                                            99-054875

Produced and designed in the United States of America by the
Fathers and Brothers of the Society of St. Paul,
2187 Victory Boulevard, Staten Island, New York 10314-6603,
as part of their communications apostolate.

ISBN: 0-8189-0835-1

Printing Information:

| Current Printing - first digit | 1 | 2 | 3 | 4 | 5 | 6 | 7 | 8 | 9 | 10 |

Year of Current Printing - first year shown

| 2000 | 2001 | 2002 | 2003 | 2004 | 2005 | 2006 | 2007 | 2008 | 2009 |

Contents

Biblical Abbreviations

OLD TESTAMENT

Genesis	Gn	Nehemiah	Ne	Baruch	Ba
Exodus	Ex	Tobit	Tb	Ezekiel	Ezk
Leviticus	Lv	Judith	Jdt	Daniel	Dn
Numbers	Nb	Esther	Est	Hosea	Ho
Deuteronomy	Dt	1 Maccabees	1 M	Joel	Jl
Joshua	Jos	2 Maccabees	2 M	Amos	Am
Judges	Jg	Job	Jb	Obadiah	Ob
Ruth	Rt	Psalms	Ps	Jonah	Jon
1 Samuel	1 S	Proverbs	Pr	Micah	Mi
2 Samuel	2 S	Ecclesiastes	Ec	Nahum	Na
1 Kings	1 K	Song of Songs	Sg	Habakkuk	Hab
2 Kings	2 K	Wisdom	Ws	Zephaniah	Zp
1 Chronicles	1 Ch	Sirach	Si	Haggai	Hg
2 Chronicles	2 Ch	Isaiah	Is	Malachi	Ml
Ezra	Ezr	Jeremiah	Jr	Zechariah	Zc
		Lamentations	Lm		

NEW TESTAMENT

Matthew	Mt	Ephesians	Eph	Hebrews	Heb
Mark	Mk	Philippians	Ph	James	Jm
Luke	Lk	Colossians	Col	1 Peter	1 P
John	Jn	1 Thessalonians	1 Th	2 Peter	2 P
Acts	Ac	2 Thessalonians	2 Th	1 John	1 Jn
Romans	Rm	1 Timothy	1 Tm	2 John	2 Jn
1 Corinthians	1 Cor	2 Timothy	2 Tm	3 John	3 Jn
2 Corinthians	2 Cor	Titus	Tt	Jude	Jude
Galatians	Gal	Philemon	Phm	Revelation	Rv

Introduction

I F YOU ARE A CHRISTIAN, YOU HAVE PROBABLY SOMETIME IMAGINED WHAT it was like to sit at the feet of Jesus like the apostles or like Mary, the sister of Martha, and listen to him. But have you ever imagined what it would be like instead to sit at the feet of one of the Gospel writers, like John, and listen to him talk about Jesus? If you could choose between sitting at the feet of Jesus or sitting at the feet of John, which would you choose? Probably the first? Ah, but wait. If you were like those early disciples, still untouched by the Holy Spirit, you wouldn't fully realize who Jesus was. You wouldn't have a clue as to what was really going on. You wouldn't see, in Jesus' miracles and preaching, all that there was to see. But sitting at the feet of John would be different. Endowed now with the Holy Spirit, John lived and re-lived his memories of Jesus. John now sees in the mysteries of Jesus' life things which neither he nor any other disciple saw during the Master's earthly life. John sees in each of them, and often in the small-est detail, a multi-layered *revelation* from God. When we read the Gospel of John we sit at his feet and we see Jesus through his eyes. That's the difference the Holy Spirit makes. And, wonder that it is, we see *more* of Jesus than if we had seen and heard him as John first heard him in Galilee.

Biblical scholars in the last fifty years have alerted us to the fact that the Gospels are portraits of Jesus. They are reports, yes, but even more so, quite sophisticated interpretations of the meaning of Jesus for particular communities of the early Church. Even the Gospel of

Mark, which used to be thought of as a primitive record of Jesus' words and deeds, turns out to be a theological commentary of great depth. This interpretive role is overwhelmingly true of the Fourth Gospel, whose author is often portrayed with an eagle because of his exalted view of Jesus and his penetrating insight into the meaning of Jesus' life. The impact of each Gospel's portrait of Jesus comes from its intense focus upon certain aspects of Jesus' life and ministry.

John's focus is unique. The plot development, for one thing, is different. Our experience of reading Matthew, Mark and Luke, where we find a sequence of Jesus' initial success, then opposition, the crisis of the cross, and resolution in the resurrection, would lead us to expect a similar plot development in the Fourth Gospel. There is, indeed, the initial inquiry by the enemies of Jesus, then their opposition and final success in destroying him. And there is a certain progression of understanding on the part of the disciples. But John's high Christology leads him to insist that Jesus knows ahead of time what is going to happen, which reduces the element of surprise in the plot development. Moreover, although there is movement in the overall story, each unit is in a way a self-contained cameo of the entire Gospel. For example, the first disciples appear already to know Jesus as the Lamb of God, the Messiah, Son of God and King of Israel (1:35-49), whereas we know from elsewhere that these titles were given to Jesus in their fullest meaning only after the resurrection. The encounter with Nicodemus, the Samaritan woman, the man born blind, and the raising of Lazarus each lead to a confession or a revelation of who Jesus is.

It turns out, then, that the major elements of John's Gospel, the seven signs in particular, are less like the steps of a mounting plot and more like petals of a flower or, better, like the avenues of Washington, D.C., that converge on the capitol. Each unit cryptically contains and points to the central mystery of the "Book of Glory" which begins in chapter 13. But each converging avenue is also a two-way street. It not only leads to the central mystery but at the same time flows from it as an interpretation of some aspect of the mystery. For example, the raising of Lazarus tells us that Jesus' resurrection is the promise and principle of our own. The Cana story tells us that at his hour of glory Jesus will provide the new wine of the Messianic wedding feast. Thus, although the characters in each story are not fully aware of what is happening, the author allows us, the readers, to join him in viewing the event from the perspective of the resurrection and the gift of the Paraclete.

How did this approach come about? John's Gospel in its present form was written only after a long period in which these stories were used in catechesis and liturgy, where they were mined for their meaning in the ongoing Christian life of the community. Thus, since the whole Gospel could hardly be read at one sitting, the reader or listener would be provided with enough information in each story to experience the whole kerygma and appropriately respond to it.

In this book, after exploring the identity of the Beloved Disciple, I seek to capture six facets of his vision: his own mysterious identity, the experience of meeting Jesus, Jesus' gift of the Holy Spirit, communion, the gift of Mary, and the writer's approach to evangelization. There are lights of other New Testament writers that could be explored about these themes, but the vision of the Fourth Gospel is so rich that I limit myself only to occasional references to the other Gospels which highlight, either by comparison or contrast, the particular view of the Beloved Disciple. I want the reader to experience the impact of the Beloved Disciple's vision of Jesus without complicating it by other approaches, however powerful they might be in their own right.

At the end of each sub-section, I provide questions for the reader. These can be profitably used for the reader's personal reflection or for group sharing, which can be particularly enriching. Any community that shares that spirituality today can experience the power, the joy and the challenge of the "disciple whom Jesus loved" and in so doing can become, in our day and time, the Community of the Beloved Disciple.

1

Who is the Beloved Disciple?

MOST CHRISTIANS TODAY UNDERSTAND THE APOSTLE JOHN, THE EVANgelist and the Beloved Disciple, to be one and the same person. It is a long tradition going back to Saint Irenaeus at the end of the second century. He attributes the Fourth Gospel to the Beloved Disciple: "John, the disciple of the Lord, who leaned on his breast, also published the Gospel while living at Ephesus in Asia." By "John" Irenaeus probably meant one of the Twelve, John the Son of Zebedee. This triple identification of the Beloved Disciple, John the Apostle and the fourth evangelist, which has been the mainstream of the tradition, has been questioned by modern scholars. The Gospel itself indicates that at least its concluding lines were written by someone else, for the "we" of 21:24 is distinct from the Beloved Disciple, and the text suggests that the disciple is dead (21:22-23). But the same text says that it is the Beloved Disciple "who has written these things, and we know that his testimony is true" (21:24). "Written," of course, in those days did not necessarily mean personally inscribing the text. Paul's letters were mostly written by secretaries at his dictation and certainly with his signature of approval. And "author" quite often means the *authority* behind a text or tradition, which could have been recorded, even developed, by someone else, sometimes during the "author's" lifetime with his approval, sometimes after his death.

That such was the case with the fourth Gospel is strongly suggested by one of the earliest listings of canonical books, the Muratorian fragment, dating from around 170 A.D., stating that John "related all things in his own name, aided by the revision of all." What is most plausible is that the Beloved Disciple had a school of intimate disciples, all of whom shared the same vision. Over the nearly seventy years since the death and resurrection of Jesus, the Johannine community lived, pondered and applied the events now related in the Gospel. Evangelization, preaching, instruction of converts, liturgy, prayer, suffering — all were part of the mix that continually drew new meaning from the central events of Jesus' life. While the final work is certainly that of an individual, it is impossible to imagine that he worked in isolation. So we can say that the Fourth Gospel is the testament of the community of the Beloved Disciple. Thus, whoever actually put together the Gospel as we have it, the work itself tell us that it records the memories, the vision and the theology of the Beloved Disciple, who, though anonymous, is the hero of the Gospel.

The Disciple — Anonymous and Universal

This anonymity is a problem for some commentators. Though tradition has assigned the Fourth Gospel to John, the only John mentioned by name in it is John the Baptizer. Twenty times! Obviously the author considers the Baptizer important. The only other person mentioned more often is Peter, the leader of the Twelve. If the tradition understood the author to be John, son of Zebedee, who was an apostle, one of the Twelve, it is amazing that he never once appears by name in the Gospel itself. This mysterious absence has led a number or scholars to say that the son of Zebedee could not possibly have authored the Gospel. If he wanted his Gospel to be accepted as having apostolic authority, why doesn't he name himself as one of the prestigious Twelve?

Could it be that, while playing a key role in the Gospel, he deliberately chose to remain nameless? There are at least three indications that this is so. First, the question of apostolic authority. John does insist on the value of witness, but he cares little for authority as dominance or prestige. The word *apostle* never appears in John's Gospel. Disciple, yes, seventy-eight times. In John, the community is a discipleship of equals, and while there is authority and power given to the disciples (20:22-23) and to Peter (21:15-17), the author expects the bond of love, the common experience of the Holy Spirit, and the service of humility sufficient to assure order and harmony. He is moreover writing for a community that knows him well and would not need to be reassured of his apostolic authority, as an unfamiliar audience might be. This is suggested by the well-supported reading of 20:31, which implies that the Gospel was written for a community that already believed in Jesus: "These things [which Jesus did] are written that you may continue to believe that Jesus is the Messiah, the Son of God, and that believing you may have life in his name."

Secondly, the anonymity, obviously deliberate, provides an excellent rhetorical technique. In Jewish tradition the naming of children was a matter of highest importance. The name stood for the person (hence respect for God's name is respect for God). And when God gives a name it signifies a divine mission (for example, "Abraham" is to be the father of a people; "Peter," the rock on which the Church is built). But there is a shadow side to naming, especially if it is a self-made name. The builders of the tower of Babel shouted, "Let us make a name for ourselves!" (Gn 11:4). John's avoidance of a name for the beloved disciple must therefore have a theological meaning. He is not an unlettered rustic. He is a theologian who is a mystic and a poet. With subtleties and symbols he teases the reader into involvement with the story. Part of that involvement is to wonder, from the first appearance of this unnamed "other disciple," who he is. Early in the Gospel (1:35-40) John the Baptist is standing with two disciples. When Jesus passes by the Baptist exclaims, "Look, there is the Lamb of God." The two disciples then follow Jesus, who turns around and asks them, "What are you looking for?" And they ask, "Rabbi [for the moment they think of him only as a teacher], where are you staying?" He invites them to come and see, and they stay with him that day. Verse 40 then tells us that one of the disciples was named Andrew. But we aren't told who the other disciple is. A careful reader will wonder. And that's just what the writer of the Gospel wants the reader to do. Later this disciple (still unnamed) is the one who manages to get Peter admitted to the court of the high priest during Jesus' trial. And then, once we are told that "Jesus, having loved his own, loved them to the end," the disciple is described as the one "whom Jesus loved" — six times! The reader begins to wonder why this title is more important than his name.

The key, which the reader is teased into discovering, is that for the ideal disciple the only thing that matters, the only thing that gives the disciple his identity, is not his name but the fact that Jesus loves him. The disciple is less a mirror of Jesus than a window through which the love of Jesus shines. This orientation to the Other is also characteristic of Mary, the mother of Jesus. She is not named either except as "the mother of Jesus." Her whole being is focused on her son.

We touch here for the first time in our meditations the relational dimension of John's Gospel. Jesus is understandable only as related to the Father, the Holy Spirit only as related to the Father and the Son, Mary as mother to Jesus, the disciple as loved by the Lord.

Thirdly, the fact that the disciple is unnamed also invites the reader to place himself or herself into the story as the beloved. Any reader-disciple can do that. The unnamed disciple is a little like the "empty set" in mathematics. It is a category waiting to be filled. We are invited to place ourselves in the story.

What Makes Me, Me?

And what challenge do we find there, we who live at the beginning of the third millennium? Where do we get our identity? When we first meet someone and want to converse, what are the first three questions we ask? "What is your name? Where are you from? What do you do?" These are the terms in which our culture defines identity. Our *name*: Dale Carnegie learned, and subsequently taught, that the sweetest word in anyone's language is the person's name. Even though our parents could have called us by any other sound, the one they gave us stuck. Romeo's "What's in a name? A rose by any other name would smell as sweet" may be true, but if my name is Rose, you'd better respect it! Our *origin*: Whether it's son of Zebedee or the town we were born in or the places we have lived, where we come from gives us a certain ground on which to stand. Can you imagine us responding to the question, "Where are you from?" with "Nowhere!" or "It doesn't matter!" Finally, our work, our job. In big institutions like corporations or universities, people are often identified by their roles. That's fine if you have an "important" role, if you are high up in the pecking order of the institution. But what if you're not? You become aware of a subtle but very real caste system, in which you are "low caste," particularly if your task is menial. So much have we thought of our identity in terms of our job, our productivity, our achievements! But what happens when we are no longer able to do those things? What happens when we get a stroke or M.S. and we can no longer command approval and appreciation because of what we do? If that is our only source of identity, we're in for a good dose of depression — and only because we've sought our identity in something that slips through our hands.

While making a retreat in Guelph, Ontario, I noticed an aging Jesuit priest who had a slight limp, possibly due to a stroke. Someone told me he had had a brilliant career, that he had served in Japan and as a major superior in Rome. Child of our achievement culture, I one day asked him, "And what do you do now, Father?" His answer stunned me: "I say my prayers and wait." A Marianist brother who was extremely active and popular as a high school teacher and counselor went through a painful crisis when forced to retire. He found himself residing on a University campus where at socials he would often be asked, "And what do you do here?" He had a hard time saying "nothing" and he eventually found himself replying: "I loiter with a purpose." And indeed he did. He just met and talked with people on campus and quickly became known for his wonderful, cheerful ministry of presence, sought out especially by students when they needed someone to talk to or a shoulder to cry on.

Putting our identity on "where we come from" or on knowing famous people whose names we can drop, or on what we have done previously, or on our present achievements or rank, can be destructive of community by leading to a spirit of competition, a "one-upmanship." Our culture is infected with that virus.

But what if everyone decided that their real identity comes from the fact that they are loved, and loved by the Lord so much as to be called his beloved? What if we let go of all those other shaky foundations of identity? Wouldn't we delight in promoting and encouraging others? Wouldn't we become enablers instead of competitors? In the Gospel of John, the disciple who never names himself delights in naming and spotlighting others: Peter, Andrew, Philip, Nathanael, Lazarus, Mary, Martha, Judas Iscariot and the other Judas (14:22). That's what happens when we know we are loved. The ego ceases to be a billiard ball knocking others out of the way and becomes instead a unifier.

Thus the anonymous disciple fosters that communion which Jesus prays for in 17:21, "that they all may be one, as you, Father, are in me and I in you, that they may be in us." Or again in 1 John 1:3: "that you may have fellowship with us and our fellowship may be with the Father and with his son Jesus Christ."

And because the beloved disciple lacks particularity, he can stand for the universal disciple. No one can say, "Because John was a Jew, or a Greek, or a man limited by the world-view of a first-century person (or even a male), I can't identify with him." On the contrary, anyone who lets Jesus love him can be the beloved disciple.

One might ask where the beloved disciple learned this emptying of self. We are permitted to speculate that it was from that other figure in John's Gospel who is also unnamed, the mother of Jesus. For if John took her into his heart from Jesus on the cross, then surely he was shaped in his focus on Jesus by hers.

This self-emptying corresponds to what Father Chaminade called the "consummation virtues," especially those of humility and modesty. He saw this state of consummation as the goal of discipleship. In this state, the disciple seeks nothing but the glory of God and the life of charity. Like the beloved disciple, the one at this stage becomes a window through which God's love shines without hindrance. And because it does, others can be drawn into the divine embrace.

Who, then, is the Beloved Disciple? You, me, and anyone who comes to know the love of Jesus.

Questions for Reflection/Sharing

1. Trace your own growth from childhood onwards in terms of your search for identity. What stages did you outgrow? Where are you now?
2. Recall someone (keep the person anonymous) in your experience whose ego, whose "wanting to make a name for himself," blocked you or others from experiencing the presence of God? Then recall someone who had the opposite effect upon you because they set their ego aside.
3. Imagine a scene in which Mary, now mother of the Beloved Disciple, helps him through a crisis by reminding him to focus upon Jesus and his love.
4. For those who find their identity in their achievements, or who are "workaholics," the spirituality of the Beloved Disciple can

be healing because it focuses on relationship as giving identity. What does this say to you?

5. The mother of Jesus and the Beloved Disciple are not known by personal names. If you applied this principle to yourself, what "anonymous name" would you give yourself?

2

Meeting Jesus

OR JOHN, LIFE BEGINS WHEN ONE MEETS JESUS, AND SO ONE OF THE major interests of the evangelist is to lead the reader to this life-giving encounter For those who have never met Jesus, the Gospel introduces him. For those who already believe in him, the Gospel invites a reliving and a deepening of the encounter. John does this by providing several examples of encounters, as if to suggest that the ways of meeting Jesus are as different as the persons who meet him. The message to us as readers is that God has tailored our encounter with Jesus to our needs, our personality, our individual history.

The First Disciples Meet Jesus (Jn 1:35-51)

The first encounter is that of the Beloved Disciple himself — or so we are led to believe by the presence of the anonymous disciple at Andrew's side in 1:37-40. The Beloved Disciple has been a disciple of John the Baptizer. Baptized by John, he had buried himself in the waters of repentance that he might be ready for the kingdom — and even more to have a heart pure to meet the "mightier one" John had foretold. When Jesus passes by, however, the Baptizer does not identify him as that "mightier one," the title John uses in the synoptics (Mk 1:7; Mt 3:11; Lk 3:16). Nor does he call him the Messiah. He says instead, "Behold the Lamb of God" (Jn 1:36).

What did the Beloved Disciple understand by that title? Had his master earlier explained that the coming one would be a lamb of sacrifice, the Passover Lamb in human form — or perhaps the innocent lamb of Isaiah 53:7, whose life was unjustly taken away? Or was the evangelist reading the title back into something the Baptizer said and seeing it now in the light of that awesome Good Friday when the Son of God shed his blood and died at the precise hour the Passover lambs were being slain in the Temple? That is certainly the meaning the evangelist sees in the title, but probably at this moment in the narrative, the Beloved Disciple can only wonder what it means. Wonder and fascination seize the two disciples, and they set out with an eagerness tempered by awe for the holy.

Jesus turns and asks them *what* they are looking for. He doesn't say *whom* (which we might expect) but *what*. They don't know yet *who* Jesus is, and Jesus honors the present stage of their spiritual development. They do have longings, *whats*. They don't yet know the fulfillment of all their *whats* is the *who* they are following. Later, the Benedictine tradition would hold that when a prospective candidate arrives at the monastery gate, asking admittance, the question should be put to him: "What do you seek?" He should be admitted only if he answers: "God."

As with Bartimaeus, whom Jesus asked, "What do you want me to do for you?", Jesus asks these disciples to state what they want, thus drawing them to take the first step in this new relationship. They call him "Rabbi," nothing more at this point, and, surprised perhaps by his question and not knowing quite what to say, they ask what seems to be an almost banal question, "Where do you live?" If it seems to be nothing more than a conversation starter, or at most an expression of curiosity, they have really asked the key question of the Gospel. For where Jesus really lives is on the Father's breast (1:18). "Come and see," Jesus says. By coming they will not only see where Jesus stays and spend the day with him, they will one day "see" him in his risen glory and understand fully who he is.

There is much here to ponder in our call to discipleship. Rarely does one meet Jesus "out of the blue." The Beloved disciple was prepared by John the Baptizer, the first evangelizer. So too a friend or a preacher or a retreat master, a community even, prepares a person to meet Jesus. Then there is the period of searching, questioning, fascination with Jesus. One reads a Gospel or an inspiring book and a flame of fascination grows. One has not arrived at full faith yet, but there is great promise in this step forward. At this moment, Jesus may ask, "What are you seeking / What do you want?" It is helpful at this point to verbalize as best we can the hopes of our heart. Everyone is looking for a Messiah of some kind — someone or something that will fulfill all our hopes and desires. Andrew believes his hopes as a Jew are going to be met in Jesus, for he goes to find his brother Peter and tells him, "We have found the *Messiah!*" Jesus is more than the Messiah, of course, but for a Jew this confession is a great step forward. Perhaps what we can learn from this is that Jesus is for us what he was for Andrew and Peter, the fulfillment of our hopes.

We hear no more of the anonymous disciple at this point. The focus is on the rapid spread of the excitement about Jesus and the multiple encounters. When Peter arrives, he does not entitle Jesus. Jesus entitles him. In giving him the name "Rock," Jesus forecasts Peter's mission as foundation of the Church. Mission is already included in the call, just as it was when Jesus said to the fishermen, "Come after me, and I will make you fishers of men" (Mk 1:17). Neither Peter nor the other disciples have a clue as to what this might mean, but Jesus, who knows the future as they do not, sees their ultimate destiny. So it is with us when Jesus calls. We are not ready for ministry yet — we may not even feel its appeal. For the present it's enough to meet Jesus, to seek him out, to follow him. When I first felt the call of Jesus, being a missionary to a foreign land was not even in the horizon of my consciousness, nor did I, even in the fervor of the novitiate, feel so called. But one day years later I would end up a missionary in Nepal, all because I fell in love with Jesus and said "yes" to his call as a teenager.

In the first scene, it is the disciples who seek Jesus. But, like Lady Wisdom Jesus not only is available to those who seek him (Ws 6:12), he also seeks out faithful souls and reveals himself to them (Ws 6:13,16). Thus, going to Galilee, Jesus "finds" Philip (1:43), which means he took the initiative to look for him. Meeting Jesus is such a grace that one realizes, as Jesus later says, "You have not chosen me, but I have chosen you" (Jn 15:16). The hound of heaven has been after us even when we "fled him down the nights and down the days, down the labyrinthine ways" of our own ego. We may think we have found Jesus. In reality it is he who has found us. "It is not that we have loved God, but that he first loved us" (1 Jn 4:19).

The very encounter with Jesus, however, enables us to share in Jesus' seeking and finding. Philip, found by Jesus, in turn "finds" Nathanael. The latter's encounter with Jesus shows us another way the Lord can come into our life and change us forever. Nathanael is an extrovert who hardly ever has an unspoken thought. He is transparent in his honesty and frankness: "Can anything good come from Nazareth?" Though he said this out of the earshot of Jesus, Jesus "knows" him already and warmly affirms his frankness. Jacob, the first to bear the name "Israel" (Gn 32:29), was a deceiver (Gn 27:35-36), but not so Nathanael. He is the "true Israelite," the one deserving the name, one who struggles with God (Gn 32:29). Nathanael is amazed that Jesus already knows his character. He is even more amazed when Jesus tells him he saw him "under the fig tree." This is obviously a prophetic insight, a "word of knowledge." John gives us no further clue as to what happened under the fig tree. Was it a moral crisis? Was he studying the Law, as rabbis sometimes did there? Or was he wrestling with God, as Jacob, the first Israel did? In the Old Testament sitting under the fig tree was a symbol of enjoying Messianic peace (Mi 4:4; Zc 3:10). What brings about Nathanael's conversion and confession of faith is a word from Jesus that has

Nathanael's name on it, a word that strikes home as a personal message.

Our turning to the Lord, too, can be occasioned by a "word from the Lord." I know a devout woman who has the gift of the "word of knowledge." The most casual encounter in the supermarket at times leads to a life-changing moment when she asks the other a simple question that reveals something of the person's life. "How did you know this? Are you a psychic?" the other will often respond. "No," she will reply, "absolutely not. I just feel the Lord wants you to know he loves you and if you put your faith in him, he will lead you." Frequently this leads the other to share more of his or her journey and ends in a ministry of prayer.

Or the "word from the Lord" may be a passage from Scripture. Augustine was trapped in the "sweet chains" of sin. As he walked in his garden he heard a child singing, *"Tolle, lege"* ("Take and read"). There on a bench was a Bible. He picked it up and his eyes fell on the words, "Not in orgies and drunkenness, not in promiscuity and licentiousness, not in rivalry and jealousy. But put on the Lord Jesus Christ and make no provision for the desires of the flesh" (Rm 13:13-14). At that moment Augustine was Nathanael, confronted by a word from the Lord that changed his life.

Nathanael confesses Jesus to be the Son of God, the King of Israel. Again we must distinguish between Nathanael's understanding of the words and that of the evangelist later recording these words. In the original historical encounter, Nathanael may have meant only that Jesus was the Messiah. "Son of God" could be understood that way, and "King of Israel" surely meant Messiah. The evangelist, of course, understands Jesus to be Son of God in the divine sense which Thomas will profess after seeing Jesus risen. And the enlightened reader will also know that Jesus is the one due the confession, "My Lord and my God" (20:28). But Nathanael and the other disciples will not come to the understanding that is the fruit of perfect faith until they see Jesus' signs and experience his resurrection.

Questions for Reflection/Sharing

1. What especially struck you in this story? Is there any parallel with your own life?

The Wedding at Cana: Sign, Glory and Faith (Jn 2:1-11)

The disciples accompany Jesus to the wedding feast at Cana. Despite the titles they have given to Jesus, they have not come to full faith, for their understanding is still limited by their nationalistic hopes. But now, at Cana, they see his first sign. On the surface it is a gesture of compassion (Mary's first of all!) to save the host embarrassment. But at a deeper level it signifies the Messianic wedding banquet, and that is why the evangelist calls it a *sign*. It is John's preferred term for miracle, since it is not only a manifestation of divine power but more importantly a parable in action revealing some aspect of Jesus' paschal mystery. As mentioned earlier, each of Jesus' signs anticipates and illustrates the Book of Glory, the paschal event that begins with the Last Supper in chapter 13 and ends with the resurrection. In this first sign John says explicitly that Jesus *revealed his glory* (2:11). For the evangelist, Jesus' risen glory shines through already in his public ministry, at least for those well-disposed. Such are the disciples. They see his glory manifested in the miracle, and they believe in him.

One sign is sufficient to evoke their faith. No signs will be sufficient for those whose minds are closed. The book of signs will end on this tragic note: "Although he had performed so many signs in their presence, they did not believe in him" (12:37). Here is a key theme in the Gospel of the Beloved Disciple. Signs invite faith; they do not compel it. Anyone who has tried to win the trust of disturbed children knows full well that the mentor can multiply his or her signs of love and concern for the child, but until the child *decides* to risk trusting the mentor, nothing happens in the relationship. So it is with

Jesus. Having faith in Jesus and trusting him on the basis of a sign is a grace, for "no one can come to me unless the Father draw him" (6:44). For the disciples one sign was sufficient to come to believe in Jesus. But there was one person in the story whose faith was greater yet. It preceded and won the sign. Mary. Looking back on this scene, the Beloved Disciple admires the faith of the one he has learned to call "Mother." Her perfect faith will be contrasted not only with the disbelieving "Jews," but with the hesitant, imperfect faith of Nicodemus, which we will now experience.

Questions for Reflection/Sharing

1. Think of a sign the Lord gave in your life that led you to a deeper faith in him.
2. "I see his blood upon the rose…" wrote the poet, whose faith enabled him to see Christ reflected in nature. What signs of Christ do you find around you? In nature? In persons? In events?

A Theologian Meets Jesus (Jn 3:1-21)

Nicodemus is a Pharisee and a member of the Sanhedrin, the supreme ruling body of the Jews. He is also a teacher (3:10) and therefore a rabbi or scribe learned in the Law. Unlike the Sadducees who accepted only the written law, the Pharisees were committed to the oral law, that is, the rabbinic interpretations which sought to apply the Law to the minutest details of daily living. They were thus a zealous, fervent group within Judaism, desiring to live perfectly according to the plan of God. Though many of them would find Jesus' teaching and activity threatening to the point of plotting his death, Nicodemus and those he represents (notice the "we" of 3:2) are inwardly moved by the freshness of Jesus' teaching and the undeniable miracles which authenticate it. It is these signs that attract this "ruler of the Jews," but he seeks out Jesus only by night, secretly lest his status be compromised. He is one of those who, living the truth as best he knows how, comes to the Light (3:21). Yet at this point he knows Jesus only as rabbi or teacher (3:2). Though Jesus is certainly more than that, he does respond by teaching, intuiting perhaps Nicodemus' willingness to test the boundaries of his own assumptions in the encounter.

It is not enough, Jesus says, for you to observe the Law, even the oral law in its integrity. If you would enter the kingdom of God, you must be born again. Nicodemus was not prepared for that. Even when Jesus explains that Nicodemus must be born again "of water and the Spirit," the Pharisee asks, "How can this be?" Nowhere in the Old Testament was rebirth a condition for being worthy of the kingdom. In fact, such an idea was sedulously avoided lest it imply that a human being could, by divine rebirth, become a god. There were other images of the covenant union, even the bold one of marriage, but never that of rebirth. Jesus does not give a rational explanation of this rebirth. Instead he appeals to mystery. If there is mystery and surprise on the natural level, like the wind, how much more on the supernatural level, where the Spirit blows where it will. Still, this rebirth, which brings eternal life, is tied to the historical Jesus and to faith in him, more specifically to faith in his saving death (3:15).

John then goes on to explain, to the reader if not to Nicodemus, what makes possible the new birth. "God so loved the world that he gave his Son, so that everyone who believes in him might not perish but might have eternal life." And then the evangelist returns to the light and darkness theme with which the scene opened when Nicodemus came to Jesus by night: "This is the verdict, that the light came into the world, but people preferred darkness to light, because their works were evil. For everyone who does wicked things hates the light and does not come toward the light, so that his works might not be exposed. But whoever lives the truth comes to the light, so that his works may be clearly seen as done in God" (3:19-21).

The story ends with Nicodemus standing there. Does he retreat from the Light back into the shadows? Is Jesus too much for him? We don't know — because John invites us to decide what *we* would do. If we look at our past, we notice a mixture of good and evil that we have done. Each of these makes a claim on our life-decision now. Will the darkness of our past swallow us back into the shadows? Or will the light of grace that was already flickering there as hunger before we met Jesus, burst into flame as it touches the Light of the world? Nicodemus, who remained a secret believer, would have a second chance, for he helps bury Jesus, bringing enough spices for the burial of a king.

What do we learn from all of this about meeting Jesus? That professionals have the hardest time converting to full faith in Jesus? That, if they do, they will be tempted not to show it openly, lest they compromise their professional image? Perhaps all of us are tempted to straddle, giving our heart secretly to Jesus but hiding our faith in him from the world. Nicodemus at least eventually broke out of the mold. He found that "if anyone loves the world, the love of the Father is not in him" (1 Jn 2:15). The flame hidden in his heart finally proved stronger than the world (1 Jn 4:4; 5:4-5). He found it was not enough to believe in the heart — one must confess with the lips and life (Rm 10:9-10). May it be so for us — sooner rather than later.

Questions for Reflection/Sharing

1. Do you find yourself struggling between your inner faith in Jesus and outwardly proclaiming it? What would change in your life if there was more consistency between your faith in Jesus and your outward manifestation of it?

Jacob's Well and Jesus' Well (Jn 4:1-42)

Once again we have an unnamed person, "a woman of Samaria," but precisely because unnamed she can symbolize anyone. In the text she symbolizes the entire people of Samaria. What is unusual about this woman's meeting Jesus is the wholly unexpected nature of it. The woman comes for water and sees a Jew sitting near the well. She doesn't address him nor does she expect him to speak. But Jesus takes the initiative, breaking the unwritten codes cemented for centuries between Jews and Samaritans. Tired and thirsty, he does not shun asking for a gift, he the giver of all. This is the woman's first surprise. The second is the sudden shift from ordinary drinking water to living water. Jesus has a gift he would gladly give if only the woman knew that she needed it, wanted it, and asked for it. Again Jesus speaks, however allusively, of the Holy Spirit. That Spirit he describes as *gift* and as *living water*. As gift: The Holy Spirit cannot be bought (as Simon Magus discovered, Ac 8:20), cannot even be merited. The Holy Spirit is gift, bestowed freely out of love. If she only asks him, as Jesus has asked her, he will give it. Living water means flowing water, water where all kinds of creatures can live. In fact the Spirit is a permanent spring of this water. The woman, still thinking on the level of natural water, asks that she may have it. It would spare her the daily journey to Jacob's well.

But Jesus cannot give the Spirit because there is a block — the woman is living in adultery. Jesus' word of knowledge opens the woman's eyes to see he is more than the Jew she first saw. He is a prophet. If she would taste the living water of the Spirit, she must repent. It may well be that the woman represents the entire people of Samaria, living with a false god when their true "husband" is the God of Israel. The rest of the conversation suggests this symbolism, as the woman wonders where the center of true worship is. Jesus replies that, although salvation is from the Jews, it is now available only in the Holy Spirit that Jesus offers and in the truth that Jesus is (14:6). Finally, Jesus reveals himself as the Messiah of the Jews and (probably) as the "Coming One" the Samaritans have been looking for. And from that moment the woman becomes a missionary to her own people, who eventually proclaim Jesus as the Savior of the world (4:42).

What do we learn here about encountering Jesus? Our meeting with him may occur in the most unexpected way. It could begin by a thirsty person asking us for a drink ("I was thirsty and you gave me to drink," Mt 25:35). But it could be that our usual sources of enjoyment, like the water of Jacob's well, no longer satisfy the deepest longing of our soul. A surprising revelation of our moral condition may occur, uncovering our rationalizations and exposing our sin. We need to repent. But more than that, we need to *ask* Jesus for the gift of living water, the Holy Spirit, the gift God is most eager to give to anyone who asks (Lk 11:13). Like the woman, we come to Jesus as a sinner and leave as a missionary. Such is the transforming power of meeting Jesus.

Questions for Reflection/Sharing

1. Think of a period of your life when you were unaware of Jesus, and then how he revealed himself to you.
2. Have you asked him for the gift of the Holy Spirit? What kind of experience does the image of living water suggest to you?
3. Conversion is a never-ending process. So too is the work of the Holy Spirit, whom we need to ask for daily. How have you experienced this in your life?

Surprised by Healing (Jn 5:1-18)

Have you ever felt helpless and hopeless? Consider the cripple at the pool of Bethesda. For thirty-eight years he has lain there not only bedridden but worst of all — alone. Alone in the midst of a crowd. No one, neither family nor friend nor even a pity-touched passerby to put him in the waters people believed to be curative at certain times. It could be that this man, though a Jew, believed that the Roman god of healing, Asclepius, would one day heal him, for archaeologists have found remains of a shrine to this god at the site of the five-porticoed pool.

The man may never have heard of Jesus, certainly never met him, and never sought him out for healing. There is one consolation in retrospect, however — Jesus knows. The Beloved disciple who recalls this scene could sing, "Nobody knows the trouble he's seen — nobody knows but Jesus." And it is Jesus who breaks through the man's isolation and asks him an obvious question, "Do you want to get well?" Maybe the question is not so obvious, because the man may well have given up any hope, after thirty-eight years, of ever being healed or walking again. So Jesus' first action is to revive that hope, that desire to be healed. God sometimes surprises us with things we haven't asked for, but normally he gives them only when through prayer or intense longing our capacity to receive has expanded. The man, of course, is still focused on his misery, looking to the pool for the healing he never expects to get.

At this point, without even asking the man whether he believes Jesus can heal him, Jesus commands him to get up and walk. The man does — he is healed. Physically at least. Before he can meet Jesus in an act of personal faith, the divine healer slips through the crowd and is gone. But Jesus later finds him in the Temple area, where perhaps he had gone to give thanks. As at the pool, it is Jesus who takes the initiative. The man does not seek out Jesus. Jesus seeks him out. For the healing is not complete. Though not every case of illness can be ascribed to personal sin, it seems this man's was in some way. Was his very seeking of healing at a pagan shrine the sin? We don't know. But Jesus knows that once healed and forgiven, one can return to the old ways and end up worse than before. Follow-up for those who have been healed is as important as the healing itself.

Oddly, the story tells us nothing about the man's response to Jesus. We miss the "loud voice praising God" of the healed Samaritan leper in Luke 17:15-16. We miss the faith-confession of the blind man healed by Jesus in John 9:36-38. All we have is the fact that the man reported to the Jewish authorities that it was Jesus who healed him. John's intent, of course, in relating this story is less the man's responses than the ensuing controversy with the authorities about healing on the Sabbath. Nevertheless, we can draw from this story some conclusions about healing encounters with Jesus. Human doctors must often learn from their patients what symptoms they are suffering and how long they have been suffering them. Not with Jesus. He *knows* our illness, physical and spiritual, and he knows how long we've been suffering from it. More than that, he knows the root cause, and if there is sin there, he knows that too. Sometimes we may be too preoccupied with our sickness and too focused on all the doctors and the remedies we have sought to think of Jesus. It may not be physical paralysis we are stuck in but spiritual. We are bitter, angry, unforgiving toward someone. It is the paralysis of the clenched fist. We don't even have the faith to ask for healing. We're not sure we even want it. But Jesus knows our misery and somehow manages to break through it. He sends a friend or even a stranger who is a Christian, who knows the healing power of Jesus, and we meet Jesus in healing prayer. Or perhaps we attend a healing Mass. Or perhaps we confess our sins and/or receive the anointing of the sick. And for the first time in years part of our being, our soul if not our body, begins to move. Caught in helpless, hopeless paralysis we begin to experience freedom, the freedom of Jesus. We get up and walk. And then comes the crucial moment. Our healing has a name. We learn it is Jesus. And then we *must* tell others that it was Jesus who healed us, for that too is part of the healing. Witnessing to others will help us stay healed.

Questions for Reflection/Sharing

1. Do you have a testimony of Jesus breaking through your darkness to heal you? Have you shared it with others for the glory of God?

Jesus Forgives and Defends (Jn 7:53-8:11)

Because this passage was not part of the work of the Fourth Evangelist (it circulated independently and was later inserted here, as the ancient manuscripts attest), unfortunately many commentators of John give it scant attention. Yet it is a beautiful story of encounter with Jesus. Keeping in mind that it may not have been known to the Beloved Disciple nor to his school, we will nevertheless reflect on it for its powerful illumination of the mercy of Jesus.

The law of Leviticus demanded that anyone guilty of adultery be put to death (Lv 20:10) and other texts indicate that stoning was the common practice. The woman has been caught in the very act of adultery; the man, equally guilty, has apparently escaped. Though surrounded by a crowd, the woman is alone, for not even her accomplice is there to share her shame and confusion. Since Deuteronomy 22:21 indicates that there must be two witnesses to sustain any charge, it is not impossible that the woman's husband, suspecting his wife was involved in an affair, arranged to have two witnesses surprise the adulterers. In that case the husband may well have been part of the crowd bringing the woman to Jesus. The scribes and the Pharisees are not bringing the woman to Jesus because they don't know what to do with her. They are doing so to catch Jesus on the horns of a dilemma: If he says, "Do nothing," he could be accused to the Jewish authorities for flaunting the Law. If he says, "Stone her," he might get in trouble with the Roman authorities who, precisely around the time of Jesus, are said to have reserved the right of capital punishment to themselves. They make her stand "in the middle," on public display, as they toss the question at Jesus. Jesus responds with great disinterest. He doodles on the ground. He has not come as judge but as savior (3:17; 8:15).

When they persist in their questioning, Jesus goes to the heart of the matter. Punishment is the world's way of dealing with evil. Forgiveness and rehabilitation is God's way. Their eagerness to punish, as well as their eagerness to trap Jesus in his speech, is not coming from their holiness, their closeness to God. On the contrary, their willingness to condemn comes from a projection of their own sinfulness onto her. Jesus unmasks what is in their hearts. "Let the one among you who is without sin be the first to cast a stone." One by one they slink away. Jesus has escaped the dilemma. But more importantly, he has revealed himself to the woman (and to the reader) as the mercy of God. St. Augustine says, in his beautiful Latin, "There remain only two, *misera et misericordia* (the Wretched and Mercy)."

The woman's image of herself has been fashioned, it seems, by the only images of the male she has ever known: as one who uses her for pleasure or as one who condemns her. In either case she is trash. But in meeting Jesus, the Mercy of God, she comes to discover her beauty and the dignity to which it calls. The sin is not the end of her worth. Forgiven, she finds the strength to believe in the better life to which Jesus calls her. He also believes in her enough to tell her she can avoid this sin in the future. Like the God of Exodus, Jesus opens a new path to freedom for her. Freedom from accusations and stoning, of course, but more importantly, freedom from the prison of her past, a prison built both by others and by herself.

Jesus, the Mercy of God, has set her free.

Questions for Reflection/Sharing

1. Who is in the better state on leaving Jesus, the Pharisees or the woman? Why?
2. How does Jesus' solution to this situation differ from those who would either condemn or condone?

Jesus, Sight for the Blind (Jn 9:1-41)

Let us look at this story not just from the evangelist's viewpoint but also from that of the man who is healed. He was born blind. For those of us who have had the gift of sight since birth, it is hard to imagine what a whole lifetime of blindness would be like. Maybe there were moments when we had to walk in the dark when electricity failed. Or perhaps, suffering an eye injury or illness, we had to wear a patch over our eyes for a time. But total darkness? Never seeing the beauty of a sunrise or the brilliance of colors, never being able to move quickly and surely because we can see where we are going? Such is the state of this young man. To be blind is equivalent to being lame. But more than that. In this man's culture not only were priests with impaired vision not allowed to serve at the altar, the blind and the lame were not allowed into the Temple. Reduced to beggary, they would often be found asking alms at the Temple gate. That was as close as they were allowed to get to God! In the case of congenital blindness, they were often thought to bear the stigma of a curse. That someone should become blind later in life was one thing; but to be born blind must be due to some sin, that of the person himself or that of his parents. The disciples of Jesus share this view.

We don't know how long this young man has lived, but the fact that he doesn't ask Jesus for healing (if he did the story doesn't say) leads us to believe that he has accepted the common understanding that there was no healing for congenital blindness. Sight once lost might be restored by healing, but not sight that was never there. That is why this story takes on the hues of a new creation. Jesus takes the initiative, forms clay with his spittle and puts the clay on the man's eyes. What is this all about, the man wonders. He knows that it was from clay that God made Adam, and he knows that spittle was often used in healing (even dogs healed their wounds by licking them). But this is strange indeed, for, assuming that he would never see, the man may not even imagine that the creation of his sight is in progress.

Yet stranger still is the impulse he feels to obey Jesus, and he does so *blindly*. This is where his faith is engaged, not in asking for the miracle but in obeying an apparently stupid command — to wash the mud off his eyes. And why go all the way to Siloam? Would not a nearby jug of water do as well? He doesn't realize — yet — that Siloam, meaning "sent," is symbolic of the one Sent by the Father, Jesus himself. Still, he doesn't object, as Naaman the Syrian did when Elisha told him to wash seven times in the Jordan (2 K 5:1-19). He goes, washes in Siloam, and returns seeing for the first time in his life.

It is amazing that John recounts so laconically the man's return: "He came back able to see." Surely he must have screamed with elation as he gained his sight. He must have spent some time just drinking in the world around him, getting his bearings and working his way back home. And there must have been a great hubbub around him. But John wants the story to move directly to the theme of light and darkness so pervasive in his Gospel and announced at the very beginning of this story: "I am the light of the world" (8:5). The healing of physical blindness will bring out the spiritual blindness of Jesus' opponents.

Who is Jesus for the healed man? He is at first "the man called Jesus" (8:11). But when pressed by the Pharisees, his testimony goes further: "He is a prophet" (8:17). The man's parents are afraid of being expelled from the synagogue, so they pass the responsibility on to their son. He becomes progressively bolder. When the Pharisees claim they *know* Jesus is a sinner, he replies, "I don't know if he is a sinner. One thing I do know is that I was blind and now I see." But pressed further, he goes on the offensive. "If you are so interested in knowing about this, do you want to become his disciples?" And then he goes on to defend Jesus, saying that "he must be from God, for God listens to the devout, and never since the creation of the world (creation theme again!) has it been heard that anyone opened the eyes of a man born blind" (8:30-33). This confession leads the opponents to expel him from the synagogue, a forecast of what would happen to Jewish Christians near the end of the first century. It is costly to profess faith in Jesus.

Jesus again takes the initiative to seek the man out (just as he did with the lame man he had cured). This is not only an act of compassion for the man who is now without community support. It is not just the kind of follow-up counsel which Jesus gave the lame man in the Temple. It is the opportunity to bring the healed man to a deeper realization of who Jesus is: Jesus is the Son of Man and Lord (8:35-38). This is really the climax of the story — not the physical healing but the coming to the full light of faith in the man who was given his physical sight. So the physical illumination is a symbol of spiritual illumination, an illumination which involves meeting Jesus, but also involves the humility required to let a physical substance like water, the water of baptism, be the instrument of that enlightenment which is a new creation. It is not a return to a lost vision. It is the vision of something, indeed of Someone, really new.

Since, like the Beloved Disciple, this man is anonymous, he can also represent each of us.

Questions for Reflection/Sharing

1. Can you recall a moment in your life when you were surprised by a grace you had not even sought? Could you describe this as a surprise meeting with Jesus?
2. If you received baptism as an adult, what did this experience mean for you? If you were baptized in infancy, have you thought of graces you received as the awakening of your baptismal grace? Or was there perhaps a conversion moment in your later life when you "awakened" to the light, when you could say with the man in the Gospel, "I was blind but now I see"?

Meeting Jesus after His Resurrection: Mary Magdalene (Jn 20:1-18)

Mary Magdalene appears in the Fourth Gospel only in the Calvary scene and here. But she appears as someone already well known, so we can legitimately allow the information provided by the synoptics to complete the picture of this unique woman. John's interest is not in her sinful past nor in her conversion but in her role as *witness*. She stands with the other women at the foot of the cross and thus witnesses Jesus' death. Now she comes to the tomb and will witness his resurrection. The Beloved Disciple enjoys recounting this scene because he is part of the story. It is Mary's report of the empty tomb that fires him and Peter to run to the tomb. But he also revels in showing how God turns upside down the cultural norms of the time about women. Jewish law did not permit women to act as witnesses in court. But here it is a woman who is the first witness to the resurrection. It is an important forecast of the role women will play in ministry in the early Church.

Mary is not called a beloved disciple, but she surely has an intense love for Jesus, for, like the bride of the Canticle (Sg 3:1-3), she goes out to search for him. Of course, she expects to find only the tomb where he lay, for, as John explains, the disciples did not understand either the Scripture nor Jesus' predictions that he would rise from the dead (20:9). So a great surprise awaits her. The stone is rolled away and the tomb is empty. She runs and tells the disciples, "They have taken the Lord from the tomb, and we don't know where they have laid him." The we may well indicate that there were other women with Mary, but John uses his zoom lens to focus on Jesus' personal relationship with the Magdalene (and hence with us, the readers) in this scene.

Mary must have returned to the tomb with Peter and the Beloved Disciple, for they leave her at the tomb, weeping. The empty tomb in front of her is a picture of her own empty heart. Not only is she grieving at the loss of Jesus through the horrible death she witnessed on Calvary. She is even deprived of the consolation of being close to his buried body. She experiences something of what the mothers and sisters and wives of the desaparacidos experienced in Argentina when their loved one simply vanished — no body to lovingly caress in death, nowhere to place flowers, no tomb to visit. Or the emptiness of the loved ones of a soldier missing in action, whose body was never recovered. The kind of emptiness Mary feels is not the emptiness of nothingness, the emptiness that comes about because one has spent all one's life energies in sin, or the emptiness of psychological depression. It is an emptiness quite different from that experienced by the others in the Gospel prior to their encounter with Jesus. This is the emptiness of the loss of the beloved. It is one thing to know the darkness of not knowing God, of never having met him. It is quite another to have met him, to have fallen in love with him, and then to experience losing him. It is the anguish of the bride in the Canticle who wonders where her beloved has gone. It is the anguish of the mystic who suddenly feels abandoned by her Lover.

Turning around, Mary sees Jesus but does not recognize him. There was something about the risen Lord that made immediate recognition less likely than would have been the case prior to the resurrection. So it was with the disciples whom Jesus accompanied on the way to Emmaus. So it was when Jesus appeared on the shore of the sea of Galilee. And yet in every case there is an eventual revelation and recognition. Why the delay? Was it that the seer was simply not expecting Jesus to appear? Was it that his risen body now had a glory and a radiance it did not have before? The glorified body is, after all, not a mere resuscitation. It is a transformation. The interesting thing about the three appearances mentioned is that only when Jesus performs a gesture or gives a sign do the disciples know who he is. Thus "they recognized him in the breaking of the bread" (Lk 24:35). And when Jesus directs the disciples to the miraculous catch of fish, the Beloved Disciple says, "It is the Lord!" (Jn 21:7). And here it is when Jesus pronounces her name that Mary recognizes him and says, "Rabbouni." It is strange that Mary doesn't call him Lord (the title she will later use in recounting the apparition to the disciple, v. 18) but "Teacher." Probably her use of "Rabbouni" here is meant to remove any doubt in the reader's mind that the one she recognizes is indeed the same one she had known as Teacher in his public ministry. The suggestion for us, the reader, is that we be open to the surprises in our lives by which Jesus will be "calling our name."

Mary rushes forward and grasps the feet of Jesus in a loving embrace. But Jesus reminds her not to cling to him but to go and proclaim the good news to his disciples. Like the disciples on Mount

Tabor, Mary would like to eternalize the presence of Jesus, but she must release him. Her emptiness has been filled but now she must let go of the ecstatic moment in order to bring the message to others. It is not sufficient for her to be contemplative. She must also be missionary. Nevertheless the message she now carries is not a distressed, "They have taken the Lord ..." but a joyful, "I have seen the Lord!"

So too must it be with us. Once we have "seen" the Lord, that is, experienced a personal meeting with him, we also are sent to tell others about it. And that is not just that we have met the Lord but that whoever becomes a disciple of Jesus is now related to Jesus as brother and sister, because the Father of Jesus is now our Father, the God of Jesus is now our God.

This whole story is a great lesson in loving, holding, and letting go. The engine that makes Mary and the disciples run is love, the kind of love that searches. There are times in our lives, even after we have met the Lord, when he seems to have left us. This is a precious time of purification, for it is an invitation to seek him more earnestly. But once we have found him again it is important that we not cling to the consolation when the Lord wants us to move on and become his witnesses to others who have yet to find him.

Questions for Reflection/Sharing

1. Have you experienced a sense of "losing" Jesus after a period of intimacy with him? What was it like? What did you do about it?
2. Are there times when you felt the Lord "pushing you out of the nest" to take the good news to others?

Meeting Jesus after the Resurrection: Thomas (Jn 20:24-29)

The whole purpose of this story is contained in the last line: "Blessed are those who have not seen and have believed." Thomas wants proof of the kind that will leave no room for doubt. Genuine faith consists in trust of the other *without* having rational proof. And in the case of everyone after the Twelve, this also consists in believing the witness of those who had seen Jesus risen. Not being with the Twelve when Jesus first appeared to them, Thomas did not have "hands-on" experience of the risen Lord. And he does not trust that the others have really seen him as they claim they have. Jesus does not punish Thomas for this attitude. Instead he mercifully accommodates himself to it, inviting Thomas to touch his hands and side. Jesus thus offers Thomas healing and reconciliation. He does so by inviting Thomas to touch his hands and his side, the wounds whose marks are still there in Jesus' glorified body. When Thomas does so his disbelief vanishes and he makes the most profound confession of anyone in the Gospel, "My Lord and my God!" The mysterious prophecy of Isaiah 52-53 had said of the Suffering Servant, "By his wounds we are healed." Jesus' wounds, far from being erased by the resurrection, become now instruments of healing for others, and first of all for Thomas. But a broader lesson is given to the reader: Thomas believed because he saw the risen Lord; more blessed are those who believe without seeing.

The Beloved Disciple recounts this scene to drive home a point he has made throughout the Gospel: that God gives enough *signs* to evoke faith. Those who are disposed to believe need only one sign (the disciples at Cana came to initial faith in Jesus by seeing one sign, Jesus' first). No number of signs will convince those whose minds are closed to faith (12:37). The sign which should have been sufficient for Thomas was the testimony of those who *had* seen Jesus, the sign that will be given to succeeding generations of the Church. Jesus accommodated himself to Thomas' doubt by giving him the sign of his glorious wounds. Touching Jesus' wounds, Thomas knows that the glorious figure before him is the same Jesus he had followed during the public ministry and then abandoned in Gethsemane when the authorities came to arrest him.

The Beloved Disciple, however, came to believe on the basis of a different sign, a less dramatic one: the headpiece folded up by it-self at the empty tomb: "He saw and believed." What did he see? Not the risen Lord as the Twelve would see him; rather he saw a simple folded napkin, a sign that the body was not stolen, as Mary had sup-posed, for thieves would not have taken the care to carefully fold the headpiece. The Beloved Disciple does not need to touch the wounded hands and side of Jesus, the sign given to Thomas. He knows the love Jesus has for him without having to probe the wounds. Know-ing Jesus' love for him makes it easy to see a mere folded napkin and believe that his Lord is risen. That he should be given that measure of faith, more than that of Peter and the other disciples, he must surely have seen as an additional sign of Jesus' love.

Questions for Reflection/Sharing

1. How would you express in your own words the relationship between faith and signs? What is the difference between a *sign* and a *proof*?
2. What kinds of signs of the risen Lord are available today? Is the Church such a sign?
3. What signs of the risen Lord have you experienced in your life?

Meeting Jesus after the Resurrection: The Disciples and Peter (Jn 21:1-23)

Thomas, whom we just considered, is with other disciples in this story. But the evangelist is more interested here in two of the other disciples: Peter and the Beloved Disciple. Again we notice that Jesus cannot be recognized at first. But then he provides a sign. At his bidding the disciples, who have caught nothing all night, cast the net to the right side of the boat and make an enormous haul of fish. It is the Beloved Disciple who, again, sees the Lord's self-revelation in this sign. He is the first to identify Jesus: "It is the Lord!" And the evangelist, by noting that this is the same disciple who leaned on Jesus' breast at the Last Supper, suggests again that it is the awareness of Jesus' love that enables him to *see* what others do not. It is from the Beloved Disciple that Peter understands that it is Jesus, for Peter *hears* that it is the Lord. Hears from whom? The Beloved Disciple. In the race to the tomb the Beloved Disciple had run faster but then allowed Peter to go in first. Here Peter, on the word of the disciple, goes first with reckless abandon, fired by the love of Jesus which Jesus soon will ask him to voice: "Simon, do you love me?" It appears from the way the evangelist tells the story that the other disciples do not recognize Jesus for themselves until they meet him on the shore, for it is at this point that we learn that none of the disciples dare ask Jesus who he is "because they realized it was the Lord." Jesus has prepared breakfast for them. As in the Emmaus story in Luke, Jesus reveals himself to the disciples at a meal. It is possible that the evangelist wants to evoke the symbolism of the Eucharist, for it was precisely in the context of feeding others with bread and fish that Jesus had earlier spoken about feeding believers with his flesh and blood (chapter 6). The meal itself, made of the fish just caught, is the completion of the sign, just as the Eucharist completes and celebrates all the other signs the Lord gives us in our lives. God's actions in our daily lives, the routine and the surprises, are meant to draw us to Jesus at the table he has set for us.

After the meal, Jesus leads Peter in a personal healing of memories. Peter has no doubt felt a crushing, paralyzing guilt for denying the Lord during his passion — three times. Jesus has wounds in his glorious body, but Peter has wounds in his heart. Jesus, however, does not probe Peter's wounds. Peter already knows them too well. Peter knows that Jesus forgives, but he feels so unworthy, so self-condemning, that he cannot even look at Jesus, much less voice his plea for forgiveness. He cannot yet forgive himself! At this point Jesus proves his savior. "Simon, son of John" he begins, addressing Peter by his human name that recalls all that he was before Jesus called him, and all that he humanly proved to be during the passion. But then Jesus asks only, "Do you love me?" Peter is surprised by the question. Jesus could have asked a more probing, more painful one, such as, "Why did you deny me?" But no. Jesus only wants to know one thing, "Do you love me?" Peter, with tears we may well imagine are in his eyes, says, "Yes, Lord, you know that I love you." And then, surprise heaped on surprise, Jesus says, "Feed my sheep." Peter remembers Jesus has chosen him to be the rock, Cephas, the Simon renamed Peter. Unworthy of the title and the office by his own behavior, he is now made worthy of it by love. The threefold question of Jesus, evoking Peter's threefold confession of love, heals the threefold denial and cradles the Church hereafter in the forgiven sin and the healed wounds of Peter. The mother of Jesus may be the sinless model of the Church "without spot or wrinkle," but the visible Church on earth must never forget that it is built on a forgiven sinner.

Jesus then prophesies in an oblique way the kind of death by which Peter would show his loyalty to Jesus. As Jesus leaves the site of the meal, he says to Peter, "Follow me," and Peter follows. But behind him (again respecting the leadership of Peter) follows the Beloved Disciple, whose role at the Last Supper is again underlined. Peter asks Jesus, "What about him?", meaning, "Will this happen to him too?" Jesus answers that it's not up to Peter to know that: "If I want him to remain until I come, what concern is it of yours? You follow me." This saying of Jesus led the disciples, those present and those to come, to speculate that the Beloved Disciple would not die. But the evangelist (who in our view is the Beloved Disciple himself) insists that Jesus did not say he would not die but only, "What if...?" The tradition is that John, the Beloved, lived to a ripe old age and, unlike the other apostles, did not die a martyr's death.

So this long scene ends with the Beloved Disciple just as it began with his recognizing Jesus. The scene with Peter is sandwiched between. There is obviously a remarkable relationship between the Beloved Disciple and Peter. Peter motions to him at the Last Supper, to ask Jesus who the betrayer would be. Then the two run together to the tomb, the Beloved Disciple arriving first but allowing Peter to enter first. And here the two are again closely related — both in the boat at the beginning of the scene and at the end. We know from the Acts of the Apostles that Peter and John were closely related in the early days of their ministry in Jerusalem (see Ac 3:1-26; 4:1-31; 8:14-17). All this suggests that the communities of Peter and John had a close relationship. John respects and upholds Peter's primacy of authority but claims for himself the primacy of love.

Questions for Discussion/Sharing

1. It has been said, "The heart sees what the mind cannot." How does this apply to the Beloved Disciple? To our lives?
2. Office and hierarchy in the Church are often seen merely in the categories of power. How does this scene correct such a view? What should be the ambition of a Beloved Disciple?

3

Jesus Gives Us the Holy Spirit

T O MEET JESUS IS TO FIND LIFE: "I HAVE COME THAT THEY MAY HAVE life, and have it in abundance" (Jn 10:10). But to be life-giving our meeting with him must also be an act of faith in who Jesus is, Son of God and Savior. There were many in Jesus' day who could say they had "met" Jesus; they had "seen" him, heard him, some of them had even conversed with him. But to meet him in the deepest sense of the term is to enter into a profound relationship with him. It means to accept his love for us. It means to be enlightened about who he is. And it also means that as we enter into that faith-relationship with Jesus, we learn that he has a Gift to give us, a Gift that surpasses and includes all other gifts (Mt 7:7-11; Lk 11:13). The Gift is the Holy Spirit.

The Spirit Abides on Jesus (Jn 1:32-34)

Let us follow the fourth Gospel as the Beloved Disciple progressively unwraps this Gift for us. Our first encounter is in 1:32-34:

John testified further, saying, "I saw the Spirit come down like a dove from the sky and remain upon him. I did not know him, but the one who sent me to baptize with water told me, 'On whomever you see the Spirit come down and remain, he is the one who will baptize with the holy Spirit.' Now I have seen and testified that he is the Son of God."

For John the Baptizer it is the Spirit who identifies Jesus as the Son of God. Though the Synoptic Gospels are not clear as to who exactly saw the Spirit, John is emphatic that the Baptizer saw the Spirit descend upon Jesus. Like the other evangelists, it is in the form of a dove. Since this is obviously not just a dove that happened to be flying by and alighted on Jesus' head but rather a divine revelation, the Baptizer must be remembering either the dove that returned to Noah announcing that after the waters of the flood had subsided new life had begun (Gn 8:8-12), or the image of the Spirit of God hovering over the waters of creation like a mother-bird (Gn 1:2). In either case the dove signals that over the waters of the Jordan a new creation is beginning. God is creating the world anew, beginning with Jesus' baptism. Though only the beginning, Jesus' baptism has cosmic significance. His baptism contains the secret for remaking the world.

Only in John's Gospel are we told (twice) that the Baptizer saw the Spirit *remain* on Jesus. John focuses on the Spirit's abiding presence upon Jesus. The Spirit came not just in a passing way, as if his purpose was only to show momentarily who Jesus was. The word *remain* is sometimes translated *abide* or *dwell*. It is a favorite of John's, appearing in his Gospel and his letters more than anywhere else in the New Testament. The Father abides in Jesus (14:10); Jesus abides in the love of the Father (15:9); Jesus will abide in the faithful disciples (15:4) and they are to abide in him (6:56), in his love (15:9), in his word (8:31; 15:7) and through the Eucharist (6:56). Thus in this scene we are already introduced to the Trinity. If we really want to know Jesus as the Baptizer knows him, we will see Jesus at all times filled with the Holy Spirit and thus manifested as the Son of God.

John says that Jesus will baptize with the Holy Spirit. That means that somehow the Spirit that is upon Jesus in a permanent

way will be given to us. We must read on if we are to find out what
that means.

Questions for Reflection/Discussion

1. If the Holy Spirit rests, abides, remains on Jesus, does the same
   apply to you?
2. How does the difference between a gift and the awareness of a
   gift apply to you?
3. Does this scene give us any insight about your prayer?
4. If the Holy Spirit shows Jesus to be the Son of God, does the
   Spirit also show us to be God's children (see Gal 4:5-6 and Rm
   8:15)? What difference should this make in our lives?

Born of Water and the Spirit (Jn 3:1-15)

The Baptism of Jesus is the icon of our Baptism, and the evangelist introduces that theme in Jesus' interchange with Nicodemus
(3:5, 8). To enter the kingdom of God we must be *born of water and
the Spirit.* As we mentioned when treating this scene earlier, nowhere
in the Old Testament was there any suggestion that salvation could
be achieved through a rebirth. And this was because such an idea
would have risked too close an identity of human beings with God.
But by the time John writes his Gospel that danger seems to be mini-
mal (although the gnostics will fall into it), so that he can make as
one of his major themes the mysterious birth by which we become
the very children of God: "To those who did receive him, he gave
the power to become children of God" (1:12). The contrast is between being born of the flesh and being born of the Spirit. This rebirth is sacramentalized in the water of baptism. For nine months
we float in water in our mother's womb. Then we are reborn in water as the Spirit that abode on Jesus comes to abide in us.

At this point in the Gospel we still don't know much about the effects of the Spirit's coming to dwell in us. All we know so far is that Jesus will baptize with the Holy Spirit and this baptism will be a new birth. But what kind of effects will this "baptism in the Holy Spirit" and this "rebirth" work in us? It is mysterious, as Jesus shows by the image of the wind blowing where it will. But what happens when the Spirit blows? The evangelist wants us to have these questions in mind as we read on.

Questions for Reflection/Discussion

1. Why was the idea of rebirth so shocking to Nicodemus? What does "rebirth" add to the notion of conversion?
2. Many Christians refer to their conversion as being "born again." How do we explain that in the light of the fact that every baptized Christian is born of water and the Spirit?
3. If you were baptized in infancy or even later without much realization of what was going on, what can you do to experience now the meaning of this rebirth?

Overflowing Abundance (Jn 3:34)

The next clue John gives us about the Holy Spirit appears toward the end of the same chapter: "The one whom God sent speaks the words of God. He does not ration his gift of the Spirit" (3:34). The elders among us who lived during the Second World War remember food stamps telling us how much food we could buy and windshield stickers telling us how much gas we could use. It was the days of rationing. On the back of the windshield sticker was the bold print: "Is this trip really necessary?" People were compelled to car-pool. Shortages were everywhere, though clearly not as severe as they would have been had the war been fought on our own soil. In the passage in John, the evangelist is focusing on the message that Jesus gives. Why should it be accepted? Because Jesus speaks the words of God. And the reason every word of his is God's word is that Jesus has the Holy Spirit. Notice the close connection between *word* and *Spirit* here. Just as we need breath in order to speak, so the Spirit is needed for human words to be the words of God. The psalmist intimated the same when he wrote: "By the *word* of the Lord the heavens were made; by the *breath* [Hebrew *ruah* = spirit] of his mouth all their host" (Ps 33:6). And Jesus will imply the same when he says, "My *words* are *spirit* and life" (6:63).

Notice here, however, that the emphasis falls on the abundance of this gift of the Spirit. The Spirit is not rationed. Later Jesus will use the image of the ever-flowing water fountain to describe the abundant, inexhaustible gift of the Spirit. But a question arises here. The text says, "*He* does not ration his gift of the Spirit." Who is *he*? Is this the Father or Jesus? If it made any difference to the evangelist, we can presume he would have said so. Hence the likelihood is that both are meant. The Father pours out the Spirit upon Jesus without measure, and the Son pours it out also without measure upon those who claim it in faith.

Elsewhere in the New Testament Paul and his disciples distinguish between the grace that saves, which is always poured out in abundance (2 Cor 9:14; Eph 2:7) and charismatic grace that is measured out according to Christ's gift to each one (Eph 4:7). John makes no such distinctions here. If he means the Spirit that the Father gives to Jesus, then surely there is no limit either to grace as life, the Messianic gifts of Isaiah 11, the fruits of the Spirit such as Paul describes them in Gal 5:22, or charismatic grace, for in Jesus all fullness dwells (Col 1:19; Jn 1:14). And if he means that Jesus does not measure the gift of the Spirit he gives to the Church, John is echoing his prologue: "Of his fullness we have all received" (1:16).

Questions for Reflection/Sharing

1. What images of abundance can you think of? How would they symbolize the gift of the Holy Spirit?

2. Can you think of a moment in your life when you received a grace that seemed to overwhelm you?

Gift of Living Water (Jn 4:10-14)

"If you knew the gift of God and who it is that is saying to you, 'Give me a drink,' you would have asked him, and he would have given you living water.... Everyone who drinks this water [from Jacob's well] will be thirsty again; but whoever drinks the water I shall give will never thirst; the water I shall give will become in him a spring of water welling up to eternal life."

We have meditated on this scene with the Samaritan woman in the previous chapter. There it was from the viewpoint of the encounter with Jesus. Here we pause to reflect on the gift that Jesus offers, living water. Later Jesus will identify the fountain of living water as the Holy Spirit (7:38-39). So we are justified in understanding the water here as a symbol of the Spirit.

First of all, Jesus speaks of the Spirit as *gift*. There is no way to buy or earn the Holy Spirit, for he is not for sale. *Gift* puts the Holy Spirit in a very different category, the category of love and friendship. At the end of his initial proclamation in Acts 2:38, Peter says that those who repent and are baptized in the name of Jesus will receive the *gift* of the Holy Spirit. And in Romans Paul says, "the love of God has been poured out into our hearts through the holy Spirit that has been *given* to us" (Rm 5:5). In 1 Thessalonians 4:10, Paul reminds his faithful that God *is giving* the Holy Spirit to them. The present tense is instructive, and it harmonizes well with the image of the ever-flowing fountain Jesus uses here to describe the gift of God. For God is constantly *giving* the Holy Spirit to us. Like an ever-flowing fountain, the Holy Spirit is *flowing* in us. In one of the concluding scenes in the book of Revelation there is a river of life [compare "living water" here] flowing from the throne of God and the Lamb

(Rv 22:1). It is a beautiful way of expressing how the Holy Spirit proceeds from the Father and the Son, like a river flowing into the city of God, which is the Church or the soul of the believer.

The Spirit is *living* water. This is instructive, for it is unlike standing, much less stagnant water. In its most obvious, physical meaning, living water is water that flows and water that fosters other forms of life, especially fish. But here it is a metaphor for the life of the Spirit which moves *through* the believer and thus provides life and fruitfulness. In keeping with all the other images of the Spirit in the Old Testament (breath, wind, water, fire), the essential characteristic of the Spirit is movement. In the Holy Land there are two bodies of water. The larger of the two is over fifty miles long and 1300 feet deep. It is fed by the fresh waters of the Jordan River, but nothing can live in it. And thus it is called the Dead Sea.

The other body of water is much smaller — no more than 16 miles long and nine miles across. It too is fed by the Jordan River. But, unlike the Dead Sea it is today just as it was in Jesus' day, the source of a major fishing industry. It is living, life-giving water. What makes the difference? The Sea of Galilee has an outlet, the Dead Sea has none.

The image of living water, then, suggests that the Spirit received must somehow move out of the person if the Spirit is to remain alive. In the story at the well of Samaria Jesus does not specify how the Spirit would be expressed, but the image certainly implies a manifestation. Jesus will later say that his disciples would do the works he does and even greater ones (14:12). This would certainly include healings, but it would not be limited to that. Because Jesus has gone to the Father (14:12) and sent the Holy Spirit, the Paraclete, everything the Church does, praise and worship, preaching the Gospel, celebrating the sacraments, teaching, caring for the poor and marginalized — all its charisms and ministries are outlets through which the living water passes to irrigate the desert and make it bloom. And what is true of the Church is true of each member in it. We cannot receive the Holy Spirit and remain idle. *Some* release of the Spirit must happen if the Spirit is to achieve the purpose for which Jesus gives it. The first expression is usually praise, but this carries over into hearing the word of God afresh and carrying it out is some form of ministry to the Body of Christ.

Questions for Reflection/Discussion

1. Tell of an experience you had of refreshing "living water." What does this help you to understand about the Holy Spirit?
2. What are the outlets that you find attractive to "let the Spirit out"? Are there some that would be difficult or scary for you to use?
3. Are there outlets that you have not yet received but would like to ask the Lord for?

Jesus' Word and the Spirit (Jn 6:63)

Jesus has just promised the Eucharist and has made the boldest statement of all: that his flesh is real food and his blood real drink. Many of his disciples, taking his words to mean cannibalism, leave him over this issue. In response Jesus says, "It is the spirit that gives life, while the flesh profits nothing. The words I have spoken to you are spirit and life." Here again, as above in 3:34, we see the close connection between Word and Spirit, a linkage we already notice in the Old Testament: "By the word of the Lord the heavens were made; by the breath of his mouth all their host" (Ps 33:6; see also Is 40:6-8; 59:21). Jesus is saying here that his words come from the Holy Spirit, and only by the gift of the Holy Spirit can they be properly understood. Though they have not yet received the Spirit that would give understanding of his words, the disciples who remain suspend their judgment and cling to their faith in Jesus, who has the words of eternal life. In due time, when the Spirit is given, they will understand.

Those who walk away take the words of Jesus in a gross sense, judging them by their own lights and unwilling to wait for further light.

The significance of this short verse for our Christian life is enormous. The words of Jesus that are now available to us in Scripture are not to be approached the way we would pick up a magazine in the dentist's office. If they are "Spirit and life," then we need to approach them on our knees, asking the Holy Spirit to reveal their meaning to us. Paul will say that the Holy Spirit has been given to us so that we may understand the things God has given us and speak of them in suitable words (1 Cor 2: 12-14). If we come across a word of Scripture that is opaque to us, we need to be patient, pray, and wait for further light either through prayer, study, or the help of someone more knowledgeable than we.

Questions for Reflection/Discussion

1. Think of an experience you had in which a word of Scripture "spoke" to you, that is, made a significant impact on your life. What made this experience different from reading the newspaper?

Rivers of Living Water (Jn 7:37-39)

The feast of Tabernacles celebrated the years the people's ancestors spent in the desert living in tents — whence "tabernacles" or "booths," meaning tents. It was an autumn festival, and during the week-long celebration people would make little huts of tree branches and sleep outdoors under them. A central ritual was that of the water-drawing. Each morning at daybreak priests processed from the Temple to the pool of Siloam and drew water in a golden pitcher. Then they processed back to the Temple toward the watergate, where they were greeted by the sounding of the trumpet (*shophar*) three times. This jubilant welcoming of the water recalled Isaiah 12:3: "With joy you will draw water at the fountain of salvation." As the priests processed around the altar, the pilgrims watched while the choir sang Psalms 113-118 (called the Hallel). When the choir reached the opening line of Psalm 118, "Give thanks to the Lord," this cry was repeated three times. The harvest was over by this time, and to express their thanks for it pilgrims would raise a citrus fruit in their left hand while waving aloft branches of willow, myrtle and palm. But the coming agricultural year depended on rain, and to express their prayer for this, the priests would pour out the water from the golden pitcher on the altar of holocausts.

It was on the last and greatest day of this feast that Jesus stood up and exclaimed, "Let anyone who thirsts come to me and drink. Whoever believes in me, as scripture says: 'Rivers of living water will flow from within him'" (7:38). John immediately adds: "He said this in reference to the Spirit that those who came to believe in him were to receive. There was, of course, no Spirit yet, because Jesus had not yet been glorified" (7:39).

Jesus here, in effect, is claiming to be the fulfillment of all that the Jewish festival of Tabernacles symbolized, especially the elaborate water rite. Echoing his conversation with the Samaritan woman, Jesus emphasizes human thirst rather than drought. And he is melding together several Old Testament scriptures that refer to the water flowing from the rock (Ex 17:6; Nb 20:11) and from the Temple (Ezk 47:1). The ambiguous "from within him" would therefore seem to apply first to Jesus, whom Paul clearly identifies as the rock from which the water flows (1 Cor 10:4), and John will portray water along with blood flowing from the pierced side of Jesus opened by the soldier's lance (19:34). And, of course, Jesus, once glorified, is the source of the Holy Spirit. But grammatically, "from within him" refers more directly to the believer. In that case the meaning would be the same as Jesus' word to the Samaritan woman: "The water I shall give will become in him a spring of water welling up to eternal life" (4:14). There is no need to choose between these two meanings, since the evangelist has left both open for us.

Do we learn anything more about the gift of the Holy Spirit here? Yes. While the invitation to the Samaritan woman was a personal one, here it is universal. "If you knew…" spoken to the woman becomes "Anyone…." Coming to Jesus means believing in him (as the parallel expressions indicate). And what flows is not a fountain but rivers, the plural suggesting overwhelming abundance (there is only one river in the Holy Land, the Jordan!). Those who turn to Jesus will not need to come yearly to Siloam to draw water, just as the Samaritan woman would no longer have to go to the well. The evangelist is whetting our thirst for this water.

Questions for Reflection/Sharing

1. Have you ever lived in a drought or experienced extreme thirst? Reflect for a moment on that experience and apply it to your soul thirsting for the water of the Holy Spirit.

The Paraclete, the Spirit of Truth
(Jn 14:15-18, 25-26 and 16:12-15)

Up to this point, the images of the Spirit in the Old Testament and even in the Synoptic Gospels and John have been from the order of nature: wind, breath, water, fire, the dove. Does this mean that the Holy Spirit is nothing more than the movement or activity of God himself? If we had those images alone we would not be able to conclude that the Holy Spirit is a distinct person. But now for the first time we encounter a personal image: the Paraclete. Sometimes translated "consoler" or "helper" or "advocate", the word means a person "called to one's side," like a lawyer who pleads one's case in court. Since Jesus calls this being *another* Paraclete, we can assume that, like Jesus, he will be a person. Jesus was the defender and champion of his disciples while he was with them. But now he is preparing to leave. After all, the Word only "pitched his tent" among us (1:14). He has now gone to the Father. But he will not leave us orphans; in the person of the Holy Spirit he will come back (14:18), for, although the Spirit is another person, he will bring with him the very presence of Jesus himself. And this Paraclete will remain with us always.

We notice, too, the tones of a conflict with the *world*. This conflict will be sharpened as we move through this Last Discourse of Jesus. Here the world simply does not accept the Paraclete. God will send the Paraclete just as he sent the Son not to condemn the world but to save it. But just as there were those who rejected Jesus, there will be those who reject the Paraclete who bears witness to Jesus. These prefer the darkness to the light, and that choice is what makes the world *the world* in John's pejorative sense. The "Spirit of Truth" does not mean truth in a theoretical sense, nor even primarily in the moral sense of truthfulness. In the Qumran literature the word refers to an angelic spirit who helps the sons of light in their struggle against the powers of darkness led by the spirit of falsehood. This militant angel is probably identical with Michael. Here, then, the Spirit of Truth means a militant spirit.

The reason why the disciples can recognize the Paraclete and the Paraclete's activity is that, mysteriously, this person will be within them. That is, he will move them from within, engaging their freedom and guiding their choices. One who has eyesight can see and move about with confidence; one who is blind cannot judge properly where to step. This interior light and strength is the best weapon against evil, for it means that, even should the disciples be shackled or martyred, the Spirit of Truth will protect them from any infection of moral evil, error and sin.

Finally, the Paraclete will teach the disciples all they need to know not by giving a new revelation but by recalling and giving a greater understanding of the words of Jesus. In this connection we jump ahead to the closely related text of 16:12-15. The "more" that Jesus cannot communicate now to his disciples will be revealed to them by the Paraclete, the Spirit of Truth. From the context we can see that the "more" is not a new revelation unattached to Jesus. Rather, it is a fuller understanding of what Jesus has already done and taught. Thus he will "guide you into all truth," like a companion on a journey where the goal is that truth which is Jesus himself (14:6). He will "announce (or declare) to you the things that are to come." This could be the Spirit's gift of prophecy to the Church, but it is more likely that the verb has the meaning we find in Daniel 2:2, 4, 7, to *interpret*. As Daniel interpreted the king's dream, so the Holy Spirit will interpret for the disciples the ongoing events of their lives, particularly by relating them to Jesus. It would be the Spirit's special gift to help the disciples understand their sufferings by relating them to those of Jesus.

As the Beloved Disciple has brought us into the Upper Room, where Jesus is alone with the disciples and away from the crowds, we notice a change of mood. Whereas earlier, in the public ministry Jesus spoke of the Spirit either to individuals or to the crowds in terms of life-giving water and new birth, inviting all to come to him and drink, now the focus is upon the disciples and their future. They will feel abandoned without Jesus, so he needs to reassure them that far from being short-changed by his departure, they will be enriched. For they will begin to understand his life and his words in a way they did not during his public ministry. In fact, he himself will be with them but in a different way — through the Holy Spirit. And this Spirit will instruct them, guide them in their decisions, and defend them in every circumstance. Surely the disciples will go out and do what Jesus did — invite all to drink of the living water Jesus has to give. But when they encounter rejection, as Jesus did, they must know that the darkness cannot overcome the light (1:5), for the Holy Spirit, the Paraclete will be with them.

And so it is for us. The indwelling Spirit teaches us inwardly and, like the faith that welcomes Jesus, overcomes the world (1 Jn 5:4).

Questions for Reflection/Sharing

1. Ordinarily we think of the Holy Spirit as God's *love* (see Rm 5:5). In what way is the Holy Spirit the spirit of *truth*?
2. What does this mean in the context of our lives today in the Church? in the world?

The Paraclete, Witness sent by the Father and the Son (Jn 15:6-27)

The evangelist is leading us deeper and deeper into the mystery of the Trinity. We learn here three new things about the Holy Spirit: (1) He comes forth from the Father. The word translated "comes forth" is the same one used in Revelation 22:1 to describe the river that flows forth from the throne of God and the Lamb. (2) The Holy Spirit is sent by Jesus from the Father. So in that sense he also proceeds from the Son, as the scene from Revelation attests. (3) The Paraclete will witness to Jesus. By adding immediately that the disciples will also witness, we come to understand that it will be through the witnessing of the disciples that the Holy Spirit will act, as in Acts 1:8: "You will receive power when the Holy Spirit comes down on you; and you will be my witnesses...." The Holy Spirit witnesses first of all in the hearts of the disciples, as Paul says, bearing united witness with our spirit that we are the children of God (Rm 8:15). But it also includes the external witnessing before courts and even unto martyrdom. Because of this powerful witness of the Holy Spirit through the disciples, the hostility of the world gets worse (16:1-4).

The Paraclete Prosecutes the World (Jn 16:4-11)

Jesus did not speak to his disciples much about the world's hatred of them, because he was with them (16:1-4). But now as he prepares to leave them, he reassures them that the Holy Spirit, his permanent replacement while Jesus is with the Father, will be more than a defense attorney. He will be the chief prosecutor of the world. That means he will prove the world wrong in its judgment about Jesus. That refers, of course, to the Jewish court's condemning Jesus to death. But it also refers to all those judgments and persecutions of the Church till the end of time. The world's sin, in John, is not its moral depravity, its numbness about moral values, although that might be one of the results. The world's sin is its disbelief in Jesus.

The Jewish court was wrong about "justice" too. They claimed they were doing justice by condemning Jesus. It was, of course, the supreme injustice. And yet, ironically, that injustice brought about the "justice of God," that is, his saving purpose by which God proved himself just to his own promises and justified those who would believe in Jesus (Rm 3:26).

And finally, *condemnation*. The one who was really condemned in this whole scenario was not Jesus but Satan, for by the death and resurrection of Jesus the prince of this world was cast out (12:31; 14:30).

It is the Holy Spirit, the Paraclete, who reveals all this, to the disciples if not convincingly to the world. Like Daniel, who proved the verdict of the judges wrong in the case of Susanna, the Holy Spirit will show not only that the Jewish court was wrong about sin and justice and sentencing but that all the world's persecution of Jesus in the Church falls under the same reversal.

The Paraclete: Conclusion

There is no doubt that Jesus' words at the Last Supper about the Paraclete have a militant ring about them. They would be remembered by the Beloved Disciple and his community because they have experienced the fulfillment of Jesus' prophecy: "They will throw you out of their synagogues... Indeed, the hour is coming when whoever kills you will think he is giving glory to God" (16:2). In the light of this experience, which repeats that of Jesus himself, it was important to see the Holy Spirit not merely as life-giving water but also as the source of strength in battle. In fact, as Paul would say, even when we are being put to death like sheep being slaughtered, it is we who are winning the overwhelming victory because of him who loved us (Rm 8:36-37). The test of a Spirit-filled community is what happens to it when the going gets tough. Few of us in the United States have experienced real persecution. Our crosses are for the most part less dramatic, the kind of stuff every human being, Christian and non-Christian alike, undergoes sooner or later. To our shame, we are often felled by hardships that are trivial. But that is only because we forget the power we have been given, the Holy Spirit, the Paraclete.

Questions for Reflection/Discussion

1. Can you think of an example in your own life where the Holy Spirit "prosecuted the world" before your own conscience?

Jesus Breathes the Holy Spirit (Jn 19:30; 20:19-23)

Throughout the Gospel the evangelist has constantly portrayed Jesus' death, resurrection and return to the Father as one unified mystery. "If I be lifted up," Jesus had said, "I will draw all people to myself" (12:32). The "lifting up," of which Jesus speaks in two other places (3:16: 8:28), refers both to Jesus' crucifixion and his resurrection, which is the hour of his glory (12:27-28). For that reason we have combined two texts which speak of the Spirit in this combined mystery: one at the hour of Jesus' death on the cross and the other after his resurrection.

The Calvary scenes, as seen by the Beloved Disciple, are rich in symbolism. After all, this is the climax to which all the earlier chapters have been moving. Jesus has repeatedly promised the Holy Spirit. Now it is the hour of fulfillment, not only of the Scriptures but of Jesus' promise. The scene in which Jesus gives his mother to the Beloved Disciple we will explore in a later chapter. The detail we wish to focus on here is the very moment of Jesus' death.

How do the other evangelists describe this final moment? Mark simply says, "he expired," a gentle way of saying, "he died." Matthew says, "he *gave up* the spirit," suggesting a more personal act, a free surrender of his final life-breath. Luke follows Mark in saying simply "he expired," but prefaces this by Jesus' final word, "Father, into your hands I commit my spirit." In Luke's beautiful picture, Jesus gives over his spirit *to the Father*. How does John portray this last moment? He says Jesus "handed over" the spirit. The Greek word *paredoken*, translated here as "handed over" is frequent in the New Testament, sometimes for the handing over of things, sometimes for the handing over of persons (for example the chief priests "handed over" Jesus to Pilate, Jn 18:35). We ordinarily expect the text to tell us *to whom* the thing or person is handed over. But in John's text there is no reference *to whom* the spirit is handed over. For this reason, some translations understand the text to be saying nothing more than that Jesus "gave up his spirit," with the simple meaning that he died, albeit willingly surrendering his last breath. Other translators and scholars point out, however, that in John's Gospel Jesus is the source of the Holy Spirit, and they see at least a symbol of Jesus' death releasing the Holy Spirit to the Church. This is implied in the blood and water that flow from Jesus' pierced side, the water representing the Spirit that would flow from within the Messiah, as Jesus promised (Jn 7:37-38). Unlike Luke, Jesus does not hand over his spirit to the Father; he hands over his Spirit to the Church.

This anticipation of Jesus' gifts is proper to the Gospel of the Beloved Disciple. Luke presents the cross as the hard wooden door through which Jesus must pass to glory. "Was it not necessary that the Messiah should suffer these things and thus enter into his glory?" (Lk 24:26). For Luke, Jesus' glory lies beyond the cross. For John the door is transparent and the light of the resurrection already shines through it.

This last breath of Jesus then anticipates, indeed is a symbolic commentary, on the action of Jesus on Easter Sunday when he *breathes* on the disciples and says, "Receive the Holy Spirit..." (8:22). That action recalls God's creation of the first human being, when the Lord breathed into the first man "the breath of life, and man became a living being" (Gn 2:7). Through the cross and resurrection of Jesus a new creation has begun. The Easter morning scene specifies the effect of the Holy Spirit as empowering the Church to forgive sins. But surely that is only one of the effects, for the images of water, wind, breath and the Paraclete have suggested the widest possible effects of this new life given by the Holy Spirit.

Here then is another way in which the beloved disciple is the privileged disciple. Because he stands at the foot of the cross he not only receives Mary as Jesus' gift (as we shall see later), but with her he already experiences a foretaste of the Spirit. Just as he would believe in the resurrection before the other disciples on the basis of the sign of the folded headpiece at the tomb (Jn 20:8), so he is granted to experience, if only in foretaste, the Holy Spirit, gift of Jesus dying for love of him. The community of Jesus' disciples receiving the Holy Spirit from Jesus on Easter Sunday is foreshadowed in the little community of the faithful at the foot of the cross, preeminently Mary and the Beloved Disciple. The breath of the dying Jesus is one with the breath of the risen Jesus. In God's plan these are not two successive moments; they are two aspects of a single mystery, like the two sides of a tapestry. The resurrection of Jesus merely clarifies what was going on already on Calvary. Conversely, the events of Calvary, in John's retrospective view, clarify the meaning of the whole paschal event. For John, the cross is the tree of life already offering to those who would partake of it, the fruits of the kingdom.

Questions for Reflection/Discussion

1. Try holding your breath for longer than is normally comfortable for you. What does this tell you about the Holy Spirit as the "breath of God" given to us?
2. Jesus' life and death won the Holy Spirit for us. What is John trying to convey by seeing in Jesus' last breath the gift of the Spirit?

The Holy Spirit in the Light of the Rest of the New Testament

John's favorite teaching device is symbolism. It is as if he fears that getting too specific in his theology or reducing it to mere propositions would spoil the mystery that invites constant contemplation and ever deeper exploration. For him the Holy Spirit is co-extensive with the life itself which Jesus brings. For that reason, if we would understand all that is implied in John's symbols of the Holy Spirit we need to turn to the rest of the New Testament, especially to Luke, the Acts of the Apostles and Paul. There we will see the Spirit as the inspirer of praise, prophecy, vigorous witnessing, preaching, miracles, virtues (Paul's "fruit of the Spirit"), and innumerable charisms. The element of "surprise" in the actions of the Holy Spirit, so evident in Luke-Acts, is not totally absent from John, for he speaks of the wind blowing where it will (3:8). And Jesus also says that his disciples will do even greater works than he did, "because I go to the Father," which means that he will send the Holy Spirit (14:12). If the Beloved Disciple prefers multi-valent symbols for the Holy Spirit, it is because he is overwhelmed by the Gift and the love from which it proceeds. Poetry and symbols, cherished in awestruck silence, are the language of love.

Questions for Reflection/Sharing

1. Which of John's images of the Holy Spirit appeal to you most? Why?
2. What does it take in order to experience the new life of the Spirit?
3. What aspects of the Holy Spirit are only implied but not explicitly stated in John's symbols?
4. Why does he prefer symbols?

4

Communion

EVERY BOOK OF THE NEW TESTAMENT SPEAKS IN SOME WAY ABOUT COM-
munion. "Communion" makes Catholics immediately think
of receiving the Eucharist, but it is actually a much broader
reality. It means union with God, union with others in the Church
and the consequent sharing of spiritual and even of material goods.
The New Testament uses many images to convey this mystery of
union with Christ and in Christ with one another. Paul uses the images of the Body of Christ (1 Cor 12:27), the temple (1 Cor 3:16-
17), the field (1 Cor 3:9), the building (1 Cor 3:9) and the spiritual
Jerusalem (Gal 4:26). In the narratives of the Gospels, Mark images
the Church by forecasting it as the travel companions of Jesus, Matthew as the abiding presence of Jesus wherever two or three gather
in his name (Mt 18:20). Luke describes it as the charismatic community empowered by the Spirit of the risen Lord (Ac 2, etc.).

What is the Beloved Disciple's vision of this mystery? Two images stand out: the flock and the vine. Both are allegories which Jesus
develops at length. Jesus says, "I am the good shepherd" (10:14) and
"I am the vine, you are the branches" (15:5). The emphasis in the
image of the vine is on the individual member's union with Jesus, a
living union of faith and love that makes it possible to bear much
fruit. In the image of the flock of which Jesus is the shepherd, the
emphasis is on the individual's hearing and following the voice of

the good Shepherd who lays down his life for the sheep. But Jesus also speaks about the unity of the flock: "I have other sheep who do not belong to this fold. These also I must lead, and they will hear my voice, and there will be one flock, one shepherd" (10:16).

Unity in the Book of Signs

Let's look at how John develops this theme of unity as we move through the Gospel. In the early pages the disciples gather. While in the Synoptics, Jesus calls each of the first disciples directly and personally; in John the only disciple Jesus calls personally is Philip (1:43). Otherwise the gathering of the disciples happens through the networking of relationships. John the Baptist points Jesus out to his own disciples. With "the other disciple" (probably the Beloved Disciple) Andrew follows Jesus, and then goes in search of his brother Peter. Philip calls Nathanael. Later some Greeks ask Philip, "We would like to see Jesus." Philip tells Andrew and the two of them bring the message to Jesus (12:21-22). Certainly God's grace is at work in this networking, for "No one can come to me unless the Father draw him" (6:44). But the beauty of this gathering theme is the instrumentality of the disciples. One disciple shares his discovery of Jesus with another, and this is what evangelization will always be. I share my discovery of Jesus with another and lead her or him to Jesus. Although John appears to focus uniquely on the disciple's personal relationship with Jesus, this relationship becomes missionary from the very beginning. The excitement caused by Jesus' invitation to "Come and see" kindles excitement in the disciples to tell others, "Come and see!"

From then on the disciples are constantly with Jesus, witnessing his miracles and signs, although they do not fully understand their meaning until after Jesus rises from the dead (2:22; 12:16). The Samaritan woman probably does not become an itinerant disciple, but she does become a missionary to her people who come to faith in Jesus (4:39-42). The disciples participate in the multiplication of the loaves, distributing them and then gathering the fragments (6:1-13). Then they find themselves alone in the boat fighting the wind while Jesus is on the mountain praying, and finally Jesus comes to them and they quickly reach the shore (6:15-21). The scene of the stormy struggle on the lake must have been meaningful for John's community, for it too was struggling in the midst of the storm after Jesus had ascended to the Father. And they must have wondered, "Where is Jesus?" But Jesus knows their plight and comes to them, helping them safely to reach the shore. John is in effect telling his community, "In the midst of your storms, trust that Jesus knows your plight and will come to you."

The Eucharist: Personal and Communal Union with Jesus

Jesus' coming to his disciples on the sea follows his fourth sign, the multiplication of the loaves and the feeding of the crowds. When Jesus meets the crowds again in Capernaum, he gives them a long discourse about the "Bread of Life." Jesus himself is the new manna, the bread come down from heaven. And in the last part of the discourse, this heavenly bread is identified with the Eucharist, which is his body and his blood (Jn 6:51-56). As the crowd became a community in the bread that was shared, so the Eucharist will transform individuals into the Church, the Body of Christ. To put it that way is a more Pauline way of speaking, for Jesus stresses again the personal relationship with him effected by the Eucharist: "*Whoever* eats my flesh and drinks my blood has eternal life, and I will raise him up on the last day.... *Whoever* eats my flesh and drinks my blood remains in me and I in him. Just as the living Father sent me and I have life because of the Father, so also *the one* who feeds on me will have life because of me" (6:54-57). Although much of contemporary sacramental theology has focused on the assembly as the Body of Christ (sometimes to the neglect of the real presence in the species of bread and wine), John's text is a reminder that communion is also an intensely personal union with Jesus Christ. But this unity is also directed to communal unity. This aspect appears, paradoxically, in the result of Jesus' graphic words about eating and drinking his body and blood in the Eucharist. The emphatic teaching divides the disciples and some abandon him (6:66). It is one of the teachings which will divide the Church of later centuries. Jesus insists that his flesh is real food and his blood real drink. The unity Jesus will pray for at the Last Supper cannot be achieved unless it is found in the one bread and the one cup, the real body and the real blood of Jesus. "Will you also leave?" Jesus asks the Twelve. "Lord, to whom shall we go? You have the words of eternal life" (6:67-68). But the unity of the Twelve will be broken by Judas, whose betrayal and departure is announced in the synoptics at the very moment of the institution of the Eucharist. Infidelity, betrayal, disunity — these are incompatible with the sacrament of unity, the sacrament of Jesus' faithful love.

That faithful love would take Jesus to the cross. From the perspective of the high priest, "it is better for you that one man should die instead of the whole people, so that the whole nation may not perish" (11:50). Caiphas was thinking of the political consequences if Jesus was not eliminated. But from the perspective of the Beloved Disciple, his words were a prophecy. For Jesus died not only for the whole nation but also "to gather into one the dispersed children of God" (11:52). Notice how the Beloved Disciple thinks of the redemption of the world as a *gathering into one*. The good Shepherd must lay down his life so that there may be *one flock* (10:16). This is the *koinonia*, the communion that is salvation, a union with Jesus and the Father, yes, but also a union with others who share the same life.

Unity in the Book of Glory

If we already glimpse the mystery of unity in the public life of Jesus, we see it brilliantly in the "Book of Glory," the climactic part of John's Gospel beginning with the Last Supper in chapter 13. Jesus "loved his own who were in the world and he loved them to the end" (13:1). "To the end" refers in the first place to his death on the cross, but, in keeping with John's love for double meanings, it can also mean "to perfection," that is, he showed them a perfect sign of his love. For this statement immediately introduces Jesus' washing the feet of his disciples. The double meaning strongly suggests there is an intimate connection between the footwashing and the death of Jesus on the cross. John, who has already given us a long discourse on the Eucharist in chapter six, does not bother to repeat at the Last Supper what all the early Christian communities knew well — the actual gestures and words of Jesus, "This is my body... this is my blood." Instead we have an alternative symbolic gesture in the washing of the feet. Just as the Eucharist was a prophetic symbol of Jesus' sacrificial death, under a form that enabled the disciples to actually commune with that death by eating and drinking the sacramental sign, so here Jesus provides a prophetic symbol that interprets the meaning of that death in a way that touches the disciples physically. The footwashing symbolizes baptism. It tells us that in baptism Jesus applies his loving sacrifice by washing each one. Such is the implied meaning of Jesus' words to Peter, "Unless I wash you, you will have no inheritance with me" (13:8).

But the footwashing also symbolizes the *koinonia*, for in taking the role of a slave Jesus teaches that communion with and in him is possible only to the extent that the disciples bend down in humble service of one another. They must be willing to "do the dirty work" that a slave or servant might be commanded to do. Community life is possible when we put the other first.

The Unity of Love

As soon as Judas is out of the picture Jesus seems relieved and announces that the hour of his glorification has come (13:31). And then he instructs the eleven: "I give you a new commandment: love one another. As I have loved you, so you also should love one another. This is how all will know that you are my disciples, if you have love for one another" (13:34-35). How is this commandment new? Already in the Old Testament the Lord told his people, "You shall not bear hatred for your brother in your heart... You shall love your neighbor as yourself" (Lv 19:17-18). So the commandment to love one another is not new. What is new is that Jesus wants us to love one another *as he has loved us*! That is a different expectation altogether, for Jesus loved us by laying down his life for us... and if "he laid down his life for us, so we ought to lay down our lives for our brothers and sisters" (1 Jn 3:16). This is the cost of *koinonia,* the cost of communion and unity.

It is significant that in John Jesus says nothing about loving one's enemies. That teaching from the Sermon on the Mount in Matthew (5:43-48) must have been known to John. My suspicion is that his long experience of community life had taught him that those who can really hurt us are not the hardly known stranger but people who have gotten close enough to us to really hurt — like our brothers and sisters in community. If we cannot love those close to us, how can we possibly love the distant "enemy"? That is why community living that challenges us daily to brotherly/sisterly love is the best laboratory for loving as Jesus loved.

Finally, Jesus says that all will know that we are his disciples if we love one another. It is interesting that Jesus does not appeal to anything else but love. Disciples who bear the name of Jesus but who do not love one another cannot be identified as his disciples. When I began to get interested in bird-watching, I learned to identify certain birds by their "diagnostic" traits. A diagnostic trait is one that is proper only to one species of bird, so that if you see or hear that trait, you can be certain it was that species of bird and not another. For example, there are several species of doves but only the mourning dove has "whistling wings" when it flies. Applying this to the saying of Jesus, fraternal love in the community of Jesus is the diagnostic trait of Jesus' disciples.

Communion: Personal and Trinitarian

A little further on in Jesus' Last Supper discourse, he says, "Whoever loves me will keep my word, and my Father will love him, and we will come to him and make our dwelling with him" (14:23). While Paul speaks about the Lord dwelling in the community as such ("You [plural] are God's temple... God's Spirit dwells in you," 1 Cor 3:16), Jesus here in John speaks about the intensely personal union of the individual disciple with Jesus. Each disciple becomes a temple indwelt by the Father and the Son! The same sense of personal intimacy is conveyed by the image of the vine (15:1-10). Yes, the vine can also be an image of a collectivity, for there are many branches to the one vine, just as Paul uses the image of the body to speak about the diversity of the members, each having proper gifts. But Jesus here stresses the personal union of each branch to Jesus, who is the vine-stock. Notice how often the word "every branch" occurs and how Jesus says each branch must remain in him to bear fruit.

We would be led to think, then, that John ignores the community dimension of this life, stressing instead the intense personal union of each disciple with Jesus. We miss the "Body of Christ" and the "temple" images of Paul, the "Emmanuel" theme of Matthew, the "travel companionship" of Mark, even the corporate image of the unifying Holy Spirit of Luke-Acts. But wait! John's intense personal imagery has only prepared us for a greater surprise: the "genetic code" for Christian community according to John is the Holy Trinity itself!

This becomes clear when we reach Jesus' prayer in chapter 17.

> *I pray for them. I do not pray for the world but for the ones you have given me, because they are yours, and everything of mine is yours and everything of yours is mine, and I have been glorified in them.... Father, keep them in your name that you have given me, so that they may be one just as we are.* (Jn 17:9-11)

Jesus prays that his disciples be one. But this oneness is not of human origin and it transcends every human union. It comes from the very union of Jesus with the Father; it shares that union and is modeled on it. Those who belong to Jesus enjoy a unity the world knows nothing of. It is a Trinitarian union!

Jesus' prayer climaxes with even greater intensity and universality:

> *I pray not only for them, but also for those who will believe in me through their word, so that they may all be one, as you, Father, are in me and I in you, that they also may be in us, that the world may believe that you sent me.* (Jn 17:20-21)

Jesus prayed not only for the twelve but for the disciples of all ages. He prayed for you and me. And he prayed not only that the twelve be one, but that we today be one. And again, it is not human union that is envisaged here, though we may be certain that it would consecrate and transform what is best in human love. The source and object is the divine union of Father and Son. Earlier, too, Jesus had said that all people would know that we are Jesus' disciples if we loved one another (13:35). Here this fraternal love will show the world that Jesus is from God. How so? By the unity which his love produces in us. Jesus expects his Church, his community, to be made up of persons so diverse in their ethnic origin, language, occupations, and personalities, that the world would think uniting them in a single family to be an impossible dream. But that is precisely the miracle Jesus continues to perform in the Church — all can be one in him. That is what makes the Church *Catholic*. It is universal, incorporating all. Religious who follow this spiritual vision, however, witness to the unifying love of Jesus in an especially intense way, for they deliberately welcome great diversity in their community (or they should!) and that diversity impels them to find its unifying force in the love that transcends all human boundaries and frontiers — the love of Jesus.

And I have given them the glory you gave me, so that they may
be one, as we are one. I in them and you in me, that they may
be brought to perfection as one, that the world may know that
you sent me, and that you loved them as you loved me. Fa-
ther, they are your gift to me. I wish that where I am they also
may be with me, that they may see my glory that you gave
me, because you loved me before the foundation of the world.
Righteous Father, the world also does not know you, but I know
you, and they know that you sent me. I made known to them
your name and I will make it known, that the love with which
you loved me may be in them and I in them. (Jn 17:22-26)

In this conclusion to his prayer, Jesus adds two words: glory
and love. (1) "Glory" is a rich concept in John. In the prologue we
read: "We saw his glory, glory as of an only-begotten coming from
the Father" (1:14). This glory evokes the Old Testament manifestations of God's glory, especially at Mount Sinai (Ex 16:7) in a cloud
(Ex 16.10) or fire (Ex 24:17). In Exodus 29:43-44 the Lord's glory
consecrates the meeting tent and the altar. This glory is the visible
manifestation of God's presence. Jesus has just said that he would
consecrate himself so that the disciples might be consecrated in truth
(Jn 17:19). So Jesus has passed on his consecration and his glory to
the disciples to bring them into unity, the very unity of Father and
Son. And this is an assurance of the divine presence. (2) Jesus also
introduces again the term "love." The Father embraces us in the same
embrace with which he embraces Jesus.

In the first letter of John the same idea of communion with God
and with one another appears in slightly different form. It is first of
all a communion made possible by God's self-revelation in Christ:
"What we have seen and heard we proclaim now to you, so that you
too may have fellowship with us, for our fellowship is with the Father and with his son, Jesus Christ" (1 Jn 1:3). This revelation is light:
"God is light, and in him there is no darkness at all. If we say 'We
have *fellowship* with him,' while we continue to walk in darkness, we

lie and do not act in truth. But if we walk in the light as he is in the light, then we have *fellowship* with one another, and the blood of his Son Jesus cleanses us from all sin" (1 Jn 1:5-7). We cannot enjoy the gift of divine communion on any other basis than on God's revelation, his light, which is not just dogmas addressed to the mind but truth addressed to the way we live. And that means loving our brothers and sisters in community: "Whoever says he is in the light, yet hates his brothers, is still in the darkness. Whoever loves his brother remains in the light, and there is nothing in him to cause a fall. Whoever hates his brother is in darkness; he walks in darkness and does not know where he is going because the darkness has blinded his eyes" (1 Jn 1:9-11).

Darkness has blinded his eyes. We do not often think of darkness as the *cause* of blindness. Rather it would seem that blindness causes darkness in the seer. But I was struck by the truth of God's word when I once visited a cavern and saw blind fish. The guide told us that these fish were originally fish of the great outdoors but that somehow they had gotten into the cavern and because they were no longer exposed to light they became blind. And then he told us something even more startling: If you lived in this cavern without light for two weeks, you would become blind too! I realized that is what happens to us spiritually when we choose to live in moral darkness. Eventually we adjust to the darkness and never see light again, not because there is no light, but because we no longer have the capacity to see it!

The writer of 1 John hammers home this theme about fraternal love time and again. Those who gave us our first instructions in the faith taught us that we must love one another (3:11). Cain's murder of Abel came out of the evil in his own heart which he had nourished instead of renouncing (3:12). Since the seed of murder is hatred in one's heart, which is death to the self as well as to the other, to love one's brothers and sisters is to have passed from death to life (3:14), a life that will last forever (3:15). We really didn't know love at all until we met him who laid down his life for us. Then for the first time we really knew love. And if Jesus did that, we should be willing to lay down our lives for our brothers and sisters (3:16). That is nothing short of being willing to be martyred, and if we are willing to do that, at least we can show lesser manifestations of that love in our daily lives, such as having compassion on a brother or sister in need (3:17). For love is not a matter of words but of deeds (3:18).

In the Gospel of Mark there is a curious passage which bears much the same message. The disciples had been disputing which of them was the greatest. After a series of sayings linked together by catchwords, Jesus concludes: "Every victim will be salted with fire. Have salt in yourselves and be at peace with one another" (Mk 9:49-50). Though there is much dispute among the scholars about the meaning of this enigmatic saying, the context seems to indicate that the fire of judgment will fall indiscriminately upon all, like salt being sprinkled. But those who have salt in themselves, that is, those who live in fraternal commitment to each other will survive the ordeal because they enjoy peace and find support there to endure the worst of trials, whether this be persecution or the final judgment. In Matthew 24:12 Jesus warns his community that when times get tough and evil abounds, "the charity of many will grow cold." It is precisely then that mutual loyalty and support will give the disciples strength to endure. But to give that support may indeed require the kind of sacrifice which John describes as laying down one's life for the others.

Translating all of this into practical terms for family or community life means discovering the joy of living for others, of seeking the last place, of putting others first, of preferring to affirm others' gifts rather than draw attention to our own. It also suggests that we promote the kind of openness that begets mutual trust, that we learn how to listen. Hardest of all, it means learning how to face difficult issues in our relationships, neither pretending they aren't there or dealing with them in negative, hurtful ways. It means treasuring one another enough to confront, or as one member of my community said, "If I don't bring this up, our relationship will be hurt." This openness leads to a transparency with others that builds unity upon truth and honesty rather than on a mere superficial nicety. In short, living the unity Jesus prays for in the Fourth Gospel means striving for all those virtues that can make living together a foretaste of heaven and a powerful witness to the unifying power of Christ and the Holy Spirit. Since this kind of communion has its origin in God, and is, in fact, union *in* God, we cannot maintain it without prayer.

Is there a symbol of this unity which Christ wishes for his Church and for religious communities in particular? Yes, and it is Mary, Mother of Jesus and mother of all his disciples. To her we now turn in the following chapter.

Questions for Reflection/Sharing

1. Can you recall from your own experience a situation where you experienced the kind of community Jesus talks about? What enabled that experience to happen?
2. What of your experiences of disunity? Could they have been avoided? How?
3. Have you experienced community living (either in family, household or at work or in social groups)? How has it been — or could it be — a laboratory for learning to love as Jesus loves?
4. What is the role of prayer in achieving the unity Jesus desires for his Church?

5

Behold Your Mother

A T FIRST SIGHT IT WOULD SEEM THAT JOHN HAS LITTLE TO SAY ABOUT Mary. Only two passages, Cana and Calvary, mention her. And yet, those very passages alert us to a deep underground river which feeds some of the living water that gushes forth from Jesus in this Gospel. That river, in turn, has been fed by the Hebrew Scriptures and the seventy years of the community's reflection upon their own experience of Jesus, enlightened by the Paraclete. We wish then to look at these two passages and then at the whole Gospel in the light of them, for John's vision is available not only in the explicit but even more often in the implicit, the symbolic, the intuitive. In John we must be alert always to the symbolic meaning beneath the surface.

Anticipating the "Hour"

Once Jesus has gathered his first disciples, he accepts, with them, an invitation to a wedding. It is the "third day," which means we should get some clue from this story of what the resurrection of Jesus means "on the third day" (see Ho 6:2).

Since this story is going to be a "sign," indeed the first of Jesus' signs, we should ask what symbolism weddings had in John's mind.

Weddings in the Old Testament were, of course, a celebration of joy but above all a celebration of union, not only of the spouses but of the families of the bride and groom. Much more so than in our culture today, weddings in biblical times were thought of in the first place as a bonding of families — and through them the tribe and the nation. Whence the significance of the matchmaker, the agreement of the father of the bride, and, of course, the public nature of the covenant sealed by marriage. The ancients felt keenly that the integrity of the social order, the village and the tribe, depended on the stability of the marriages of its members.

It is not surprising then that the prophet Hosea, followed by Jeremiah and Ezekiel, would see in the Sinai covenant of God with his people a marriage of the Lord with Israel. While the surrounding peoples had a goddess consort for each male god, there was no goddess-consort for Yahweh. Instead, the Lord's consort was his people, Israel. That is why the people could be collectively symbolized as a woman, the spouse of Yahweh (Jr 2:2), as "virgin daughter Zion," virginally committed to her spouse (2 K 19:21; Is 23:12; 37:22; 62:5; Jr 14:17; 18:13; 31:4, 13, 21; Lm 2:13), thus making covenant infidelity nothing less than adultery (Jr 2:20-24; Ho 2:4-7; Ezk 16). Though such infidelity was often committed, the Lord promised to take her back in a new espousal in which he would adorn her with right, justice, love, mercy and fidelity (Ho 2:21-22). Among the material blessings to accompany that new espousal would be an abundance of wine (Ho 2:24). Isaiah foretold that the coming salvation would be a feast of rich food and pure, choice wine (Is 25:6). In a less eschatological context Lady Wisdom prepares a feast of meat and wine and invites all to come (Pr 9:2-5).

According to the evangelist, John the Baptist already sees the Messiah as the Bridegroom of this new marriage (3:29), a bold innovation, since in the Old Testament, only God and not the Messiah was so imaged. How many of all these resonances are in the evangelist's mind as he opens the public life of Jesus, the first of his signs, with the story of a wedding feast? In a Gospel so freighted with symbolism, it is hard to decide, for John uses symbols to tease his readers into thinking for themselves, just as Jesus did with his parables. Who, for example is the real bridegroom in this story? When the headwaiter tastes the "best wine," he calls the bridegroom and tells him he has saved the best wine till now — but the waiters know who the real source is — suggesting that Jesus is the real bridegroom. It is the bridegroom Jesus who has kept the best wine until now.

So in keeping with Johannine irony, at the deepest level, Cana is a story about the Messianic wedding feast. It points to the Book of Glory and radiates out from it, telling us that what happens on the cross and on Easter Sunday is the fulfillment of all those prophetic symbols of wine and wedding feasts.

We are now in a position to understand Mary's role in this scene. On the surface level, a crisis arises of the most serious kind. In the first century world, honor was a value next to life itself, and shame almost like the death of the family. A family would enhance its honor in the community by magnificence at a feast. By the same token, to run short of an essential such as wine would be to compromise the family's honor, to incur shame.

Mary may have been the first to notice the shortage of wine. In any case she is the one who takes the initiative in the situation. Like her questioning the angel at the Annunciation, she is not a passive, unreflecting person but an active responder, in one case to God's message, in the other to human need.

Her intervention is a statement of fact, but Jesus' response indicates that, however deferentially expressed, it was a request. He addresses her as "Woman," a title a Jewish man would not normally use for his mother but would use to address his wife or another woman. Here, as again on the cross, the symbolic nature of the whole story comes to the fore. This title suggests Mary's role in the Messianic banquet, the redemptive mystery enacted in the Book of Glory. If Jesus' death-resurrection and sending of the Spirit is the reversal of the primordial sin, then Mary is the woman foretold in Genesis 3:15, whose offspring would crush the serpent's head. And if the paschal mystery is to be understood as the messianic banquet, Mary urges the Messiah to provide the wine for the feast.

Jesus' apparent initial refusal only serves to point the Cana story more clearly to the paschal mystery, for Jesus says that the hour for providing the messianic wine will be then, not now. But in deference to Mary's request and the host's obvious crisis, Jesus does work the sign, anticipating his "hour." Mary's deference to Jesus appears again in her instruction to the waiters: "Do whatever he tells you." An interesting question occurs here. What authority did Mary have over the waiters? Did she just take charge of a chaotic situation momentarily, as anyone might do in a crisis? Or was she in charge of the waiters to begin with? If so, this raises some interesting possibilities on the symbolic level of the story. Is John suggesting that Mary is queen of all those who serve at the Messianic feast? If so, it can only be that her "authority" to command obedience to Jesus lies in the fact that she first of all, did all that the Lord told her (Lk 1:38). As obedience was the requisite of the old covenant (Ex 19:5; 24:70), so it is the key to the blessing of the new. If, like the waiters, we put ourselves at Mary's disposal, we can have the privilege of serving at the Messianic wedding feast that Jesus continues now in his Church. Our cooperation is no more than filling jars and drawing from them, but in doing so, we are collaborators in a miracle.

The fulfillment motif continues as John's literary camera focuses on the water jars. There are six of them and they are for Jewish purification purposes. Six indicates imperfection, and Jewish purification rites will be replaced by the new wine of the new covenant. And so the miracle happens — the host's family and the bridegroom are spared embarrassment, the wedding feast is marvelously enhanced, but most significantly Jesus works his first *sign*, giving the reader who knows the whole Gospel story a deep interpretation of the paschal mystery as a wedding feast. Mary thus has a key role at the symbolic level. Whether there is any allusion here to Lady Wisdom who provides wine for the feast (Prv 9:2-8), Mary is the "woman," companion of her son, intercessor, and model of faith.

This last point comes to light when we reflect on what John means by *sign*. In his Gospel, Jesus' signs have a twofold purpose: they are an invitation to faith and an interpretation, a catechesis of the paschal mystery. We have already reflected on the latter. Let's look for a moment at the invitation to faith.

Later, summing up the ministry of Jesus, John will say, "Although he had performed so many *signs* in their presence, they did not believe in him" (12:37). No number of signs will convince those who are determined not to believe. But one sign suffices for the well-disposed disciples to come to faith. However, there was one person who had no need of a sign prior to faith. Her faith *won* the sign. Mary.

There is no mention of the Beloved Disciple as such here at this feast. Given the overall picture of the disciples in the Gospel, however, we may assume that he was there. At any rate, if the Gospel is, in its final form, the spirituality of the Beloved Disciple, we can assume that he wants us to see this scene through his eyes.

Questions for Reflection/Sharing

1. Are you engaged in a ministry for your Church/community? How does the scene of Cana dignify your ministry?
2. What do you do when you face a "crisis of insufficiency" such as the hosts did at Cana?
3. What value can you see in putting your ministry under the maternal direction of Mary?

There is much to be learned about the paschal mystery from the six other signs which John relates. But let us take the direct route from Cana to Calvary, where we find Jesus, Mary and the Beloved Disciple.

The Hour

The Calvary scene in John 19:25-30 depicting the final acts of Jesus begins with Jesus' gift of Mary to the Beloved Disciple and concludes when Jesus "hands over the Spirit." The first part of this passage, the scene with Mary and the Beloved Disciple, occupies the centerpiece of the whole Calvary narrative and points to its importance. Of course Jesus, who upheld the fifth commandment, would have wanted to provide for his mother's care after his death. This presumes Joseph is dead and there are no other sibling "brothers of Jesus" to care for her. But if that were the only purpose of this scene, it would hardly merit such a central place among the other Calvary episodes, each of which, beyond its historical report, has a deeply symbolic meaning, especially as fulfillment of the Scriptures. In fact, some scholars have shown that if each of the little scenes on Calvary were arranged symmetrically, the scene with Mary and the Beloved Disciple would be the central one, the keystone of the arch, so to speak. So there must be a deeper theological meaning to this exchange of mother and sons. Let's look at the roles of the three major characters in this scene.

The Disciple

The "disciple whom Jesus loved," as we have already noted, has no name. It is as if he wants to be known — and the evangelist wants to underline it — only as the Lord's beloved. It is this relationship that gives him the only identity he cares for, more important than any personal name. For the same reason, he stands as a type, even a model, for every disciple. The text invites us to put *our* name there, to know that *we* are "the disciple whom Jesus loved."

To review what we saw in the first chapter, it was this disciple, always unnamed, who leaned on Jesus' breast at the Last Supper, who ran first to the tomb on Easter Sunday, who believed Jesus had risen only on the basis of the "sign" of the linen headpiece carefully wrapped up, who was the first to identify the risen Lord standing on the shore of the Sea of Galilee. Why this outstanding role of insight into the mystery of Jesus? The reason: his keen awareness of Jesus' love. The heart can see more than the eye.

It is the same love that enables him to stand at the foot of the cross when all the other male disciples have fled. He has understood that "faithful love came into being through Jesus Christ" (Jn 1:17). Jesus' faithful love has engendered faithful love in the disciple's own heart, enabling him alone to stand with the faithful women in Jesus' final hour. Like Mary, he *stood there* when the most important event in world history happened — the saving death of the Son of God. He saw and remembered the event in all its details. And in those details he saw what was *really* happening.

The Mother of Jesus

And what was really happening? For that we turn to the second main character in this scene: Mary. Like the Beloved Disciple, she is not known by her personal name, only by her relationship to Jesus. She is "the mother of Jesus." Her identity, her role is to mother Jesus, and that will forever be her role — not to draw attention to herself but to point to Jesus. Such was John the Baptist's role as well: "He came not as the Light, but to bear witness to the Light" (Jn 1:8), and he would say of Jesus, "He must increase and I must decrease" (Jn 3:30). But who can better point to a Son, who can better tell us who a Son is — if not the mother?

But Jesus does not address her as "Mother," as a Jewish son might do. He calls her "Woman," just as he did at Cana. As we noted there, a Jewish man might call his wife or another female "woman" (see Jn 4:21), but he would not normally address his mother that way. So there must be a symbolic meaning to the title here. "Woman" appears in Genesis 3:15, where the Lord says to the serpent, "I will set up an enmity between you and the woman, between her offspring and yours. He will crush your head, while you strike at his heel." Jesus had spoken of his "hour," when Satan, the "Prince of this world" would be cast out (Jn 3:30). By identifying his mother as "Woman" Jesus identifies himself as the offspring who now crushes the serpent's head. That Genesis text also recalls the role of the Queen Mother in the Davidic dynasty. She had a crucial role in passing on the promise made to David that his dynasty would last forever, for she alone, of the previous king's wives, bore the new king, bearer of Messianic hope. That is why the Queen Mother is always mentioned in the succession list of the Judean kings. As prophets and people looked forward to the victorious Messiah, they gave special place to his mother, as in Isaiah 7:14: "Behold the virgin is with child and will bear a son… Emmanuel."

So Mary on Calvary is more than a historical figure. The evangelist sees in her a literal fulfillment of the promise of Genesis and indirectly of the promise of the Queen Mother and her son, the Davidic Messiah. Those prophecies would apply to Jesus as the Messiah, Son of *the Woman* or of *the Queen Mother*. But the text in John refers to a *transfer* of sonship to someone other than the Messiah. It is now the Beloved Disciple who is son of this woman, and she is now *his* mother. Are there Old Testament passages which would suggest a birth, at least metaphorical, of a messianic *people?* Yes, there are several passages where Jerusalem is called mother not only of her present children — who are all Israelites, wherever they may reside (Ps 87) — but also of the future generation that will enjoy the Lord's salvation: "Before she comes to labor, she gives birth; before the pains come upon her, she safely delivers a male child. Who ever heard of such a thing, or saw the like? Can a country be brought forth in one day, or a nation be born in a single moment? Yet Zion is scarcely in labor when she gives birth to her children…. Rejoice with Jerusalem and be glad because of her, all you who love her; exult, exult with her, all you who were mourning over her! Oh, that you may suck fully of the milk of her comfort, that you may nurse with delight at her abundant breasts! For thus says the Lord: Lo, I will spread prosperity over her like a river, and the wealth of the nations like an overflowing torrent. As nurslings you shall be carried in her arms, and fondled in her lap; As a mother comforts her child, so will I comfort you; in Jerusalem you shall find your comfort" (Is 66:7-13).

Jesus' words to Mary and the disciple indicate a fulfillment of these prophecies. As often happens, fulfillment goes beyond expectations. For what in the Old Testament was only the metaphor of the city as a woman, in John is a historical Israelite woman, the same woman who is mother of the Messiah. *She* is giving birth to the new children of God represented by the Beloved Disciple, those children who are born not of human seed nor of the will of the flesh nor of the will of man but of God" (Jn 1:13). Obviously it is not by her own power that Mary fulfilled this role. It was only by Jesus' death and the gift of the Spirit (19:30) that she was empowered to symbolize and mediate this new birth. But her presence and the role Jesus assigns to her at this, his saving "hour," helps us to understand what was *really* happening. It is now possible for a new people to be born, a birth of God (Jn 1:13) and of the Spirit (Jn 3:5). Humanly speaking it is not possible to enter one's mother's womb and be born again, as Nicodemus plainly saw (Jn 3:4). But by God's power it is possible to be born again from the faith-surrendered virginal womb whence Jesus himself was born. He who was "conceived by the Holy Spirit and born of the Virgin Mary" set the physical pattern for the spiritual birth of the new people of God. And a real mother, not a metaphor, stands there as witness to this miracle.

Jesus

Having looked at the disciple and at the mother, we turn now to the third main character in the scene, indeed the central one, Jesus. Look at the mystery of this *giving*. Love expresses itself in gift. God so loved the world that he *gave* his only begotten Son (Jn 3:16). Jesus promised that he would *give* the Spirit to those who ask him (Jn 4:10). Jesus *gives* the bread of life (Jn 6). One can have no greater love than to *give* one's life for one's friends (Jn 15:13). Though the word *give* or *gift* is not used here in the Calvary scene, it is certainly implied. In fact, Jesus' imminent death makes the giving more poignant. The things one waits to give away at the last moment of one's life are the most precious. And the ones to whom they are given are usually those dearest to the giver. John must intend that here. To be chosen to receive Jesus' mother as one's own is a mark of unspeakable love and tenderness. Whoever receives her is a beloved disciple. Borrowing the words of the guestmaster at Cana, could the disciple not say, "You have saved the best for last"?

"Taking" his Mother

The text concludes, "From that hour the disciple took her into his own." That "hour" is a technical term in John. Jesus' hour, he said, had not come at Cana, where Mary too was present. It is the hour of his saving death. It is precisely from that hour that the disciple takes Mary.

The word "took," when used of persons, has the more personal meaning of "welcome, receive gratefully." Here it suggests the disciple's joyful response to the gift of Jesus' mother. "Into his own" is sometimes translated, "into his home" or "into his care." But literally the Greek says, "into his own," *own* being the neuter plural in the Greek, meaning "into the things that were his own." We might say, "into the treasury of his heart." There is a parallel in the book of Wisdom 8:18, where Solomon, telling of his discovery that Lady Wisdom is a gift of God, says: "I sought to take her *for my own*." The Greek word here is different but the meaning is the same. In the book of Wisdom, Lady Wisdom is both bride and mother (Ws 7:12; 8:2), and Solomon earnestly seeks her company and even to have her as his own. Was John thinking of this Wisdom tradition when he wrote that the disciple took Mary as his own? We can't be sure, but it is tempting to think so.

The Finishing Touch: The Spirit

The following verses in John 19:28-30 complete the picture, and they are best understood as a further interpretation of the meaning of Jesus' death:

> *After this, aware that everything was now finished, in order that the Scripture might be fulfilled, Jesus said, "I thirst." There was a vessel filled with common wine. So they put a sponge soaked in wine on a sprig of hyssop and put it up to his mouth. When Jesus had taken the wine, he said, "It is finished." And bowing his head, he handed over the spirit.*

The fulfillment of Scripture was important to all the New Testament writers. It is especially so to John. What Scripture is John referring to here? Perhaps the Scripture that underlay the previous scene with Mary and the beloved disciple. Or perhaps it refers to the thirst of Jesus foreshadowed in Psalm 22:16, "My throat is dried up like baked clay," or Psalm 69:22: "In my thirst they gave me vinegar to drink." In any case, he who promised to slake with the water of the Spirit the thirst of anyone who would come to him (Jn 4:10; 7:37-38) now himself thirsts. This detail is a powerful affirmation of the humanness of Jesus at the very moment he is about to hand over the Spirit. It also indicates that only upon the death of Jesus can the Spirit be given (Jn 7:39). He must first drink the bitter cup the Father has given him to drink (Jn 18:11). Moses had told the Israelites that to escape destruction they must use hyssop to sprinkle their doorposts with the blood of the paschal lamb (Ex 12:22); by associating hyssop with the death of Jesus, John is hinting in another way that Jesus is "the lamb of God who takes away the sin of the world" (Jn 1:29).

"It is finished" is not an exasperated cry of defeat, but the glorious signature Jesus gives to the work the Father has given him to do. In Luke 9:58 Jesus tells a would-be disciple that he has nowhere to lay his head. But now he does — on the cross! And finally, Jesus "hands over the Spirit."

The other three Gospels describe the moment of Jesus' death simply as "he expired" or "he breathed his last." Such is the usual sign of the moment of leaving this life — the last breath. But John's choice of words indicates that here again he sees a symbolic meaning. For he chooses to describe the moment by the phrase, "he handed over the spirit." At one level, of course, this means simply he died, he breathed his last — as in the other three Gospels. But John is also aware that Jesus was "lifted up" on the cross in order to give eternal life to all (Jn 3:14-15).

This new life, this eternal life, was what the scene with Mary and the Beloved Disciple dramatized, for if the disciple is now Jesus' brother, then Mary is his mother too. But it is only through the gift of the Holy Spirit that the new birth can take place (Jn 3:5), and the Holy Spirit can be given only once Jesus is "glorified," that is, once he has completed his saving act on the cross (Jn 7:39). So at the deeper level, when Jesus dies he hands over the Holy Spirit to the Church.

One might object that it is only on Easter Sunday that Jesus breathes on his disciples, saying to them, "Receive the Holy Spirit..." (Jn 20:22). And, even more problematic, what are we to make of the fact that St. Luke in the Acts of the Apostles situates the gift of the Holy Spirit on the feast of Pentecost, fifty days later.

Regarding the latter anomaly, Luke wants to situate the gift of the Spirit within the Jewish liturgical year, now transformed into a Christian sequence. Just as Jesus' death and resurrection fulfills and replaces Passover, which celebrated the Jews' deliverance from Egypt, so the gift of the Spirit fulfills and replaces their Pentecost, which celebrated the giving of the Law from Mount Sinai amid earthquake and fire (Ex 20:18). Luke's is a liturgical-theological interpretation of Jesus' death-resurrection-gift of the Spirit.

John, too, wants to point out the theological meaning of Jesus' death. Jesus is glorified not only by his resurrection, but, as we mentioned previously, also by his death on the cross, the supreme manifestation of God's love. John sees the glory of Easter already shining through the gore of Calvary. And he sees in the simple events of Jesus' last hour keys to the meaning of the entire saving mystery.

So when the Beloved Disciple witnesses Jesus "hand over the spirit," he also knows, at least as he looks back on that moment, that Jesus surrendered his life so that he might hand over the Holy Spirit to the Church. The symbolism of the Spirit is probably also to be seen in the water that gushes from Jesus' side at the lance-thrust, though the water might also represent baptism and the blood the Eucharist.

To be the Beloved Disciple, as the Gospel calls us to be, is then to welcome a double gift: Mary and the Holy Spirit. As Jesus was born of Mary by the power of the Holy Spirit, so the disciples are born again, becoming brothers and sisters of Jesus, children of the Father and children of Mary through the power of the same Holy Spirit.

Are we permitted to surmise why Jesus first gave Mary to the disciple and only then bestowed the Spirit? Was it not for the same reason that Luke included Mary in the Upper Room awaiting the Church's Pentecost? Would it not be in her company that one would be best disposed to receive the Holy Spirit? She, whose surrender to the Holy Spirit birthed the Word made flesh?

Jesus, Mary and the Holy Spirit are thus inseparably united in the mystery of the Redemption as they are in the mystery of the Incarnation.

There are practical conclusions that can be drawn from this scene for us. This scene, summing up both Incarnation and Redemption, embodies God's way of coming to us. It also embodies our way of coming to God. For our way of coming to God is to *let God come to us*. And that means receiving the gifts he wants to give us. In the Gospel of John, the Beloved Disciple, with Mary, is the model receiver. If the Beloved Disciple stands for every disciple, then he stands for each of us. And one of the ways this scene invites us to receive all that Jesus has to give is to welcome the gift of Mary as our Mother.

This is the deepest sense of Marian consecration. Although the term "consecration to Mary" has frequently been used, it is not the most appropriate way of describing the disciple's union with Mary. "Consecration" is an action that is properly done only to God. It means to set aside for divine purpose. Jesus consecrated himself to God by freely choosing to go to his passion and death, thus enabling us to be consecrated with him to God (Jn 17:17-18). Our consecration happens in baptism. By it we become a holy people, God's temple (1 Cor 3:16; 6:19), Christ's body (1 Cor 6:15; 12:13). But this assumes that we consciously accept the gift, and we reach the holiness promised in our baptismal consecration only to the extent that we continue to open ourselves to the gifts of God. Christian holiness involves asceticism, yes, but it is not primarily asceticism. It is primarily opening ourselves to the gifts of God, and God always has more to give us than we are capable of receiving at the moment. So we reach the full meaning of consecration as we more and more open ourselves to receive his gifts. Now the gifts that Jesus saved for the last were his Mother and his Spirit. To receive those gifts and to allow them to transform us is to reach the fullness of our baptismal consecration. So, instead of saying "consecration to Mary," we would be better advised to follow the example of Pope John Paul II and call this an "entrustment to Mary" of all that we are. Or, in imitation of the Beloved Disciple, our conscious *taking* of Mary into our lives and then, with her, allowing Jesus to breathe the Holy Spirit upon us.

Questions for Reflection/Sharing

1. What new insights have you gained by this meditation on the Calvary scene?
2. What does it mean in practical terms for you to consciously *take* Mary into your life?
3. In what way does Mary dispose us to receive the Holy Spirit?

6

Bringing Others to Jesus

THE VISION OF THE BELOVED DISCIPLE WOULD NOT BE COMPLETE WITH-
out a word about mission. For, however intensely John
stresses mutual love and unity within the community, at times
even over against the world outside, there is also the world that God
so loves that he gave his only Son that whoever believes in him might
not perish but might have eternal life (3:16). So, like the Synoptic
Gospels and the Acts of the Apostles, the fourth evangelist sees the
disciples, that is, the Church, missioned to the ends of the earth. And
yet he has a distinct understanding and emphasis on mission which
it will be fruitful to explore.

We can begin with the first missionary, Jesus. In John Jesus is
primarily *revealer*. Even as the eternal Word begotten of the Father
he was and is revealer. In him was life, and this life, even prior to the
Incarnation, was the light of the human race. The imprint of the
Word, God's wisdom and self-revelation, is found in the created
universe, from the farthest star to the least flower. And this light shines
there even now for all to see (1:4-5).

This light was not only glowing. It was growing (1:9). It en-
tered human history with Abraham and like a divine rheostat grew
ever brighter through Moses and the prophets till it flooded the world
when the Word became flesh. He was now light and life incarnate.

And the evangelist could say, "We saw his glory, glory as befits the only Son of the Father" (1:14).

When and how did they see his glory? At the resurrection surely. But just before narrating Jesus' public life the evangelist tells us that the very human story of Jesus showed forth God's glory. It will indeed be the project of the Gospel to show how this glory shone forth in everything Jesus did (2:11). Whence the dramatic line that concludes the prologue: "No one has ever seen God. The only Son, God, ever at the Father's side, has revealed him" (1:18). The English translation does not quite capture the impact of the Greek verb *revealed*, which climaxes the sentence and the entire prologue. To get the emphasis of the Greek, I retranslate it: "God, whom no one has seen, the only-begotten, God, ever at the Father's breast, has *revealed.*" The word *revealed* stands like the pin on which the top of the entire prologue spins, and it throws wide the curtain on the public life of Jesus which begins in the next verse.

In an earlier chapter we noted how the call of Jesus' first disciples in John differs from the description in the Synoptics. In Matthew and Mark Jesus walks by the Sea of Galilee, sees the fishermen and calls them (Mt 4:18-22; Mk 1:16-20). In Luke Jesus' call of Peter is prepared for by the wonderful haul of fish. In every case, though, there is a reference to "catching men." In John Jesus walks by John the Baptist, who points him out, and the first disciples (one of whom may be the Beloved Disciple) follow Jesus out of curiosity. And once they discover Jesus, they fan out to tell others. The networking of catching men, only forecast in the Synoptics, is acted out in the very constitution of the first group of disciples. Doubtless the evangelist wants to present this not merely to tell how the first disciples gathered around Jesus but to offer a model for the evangelizing to be done by the members of his community — and by us, the readers. If we have authentically found Jesus, we will want to share that experience with others. We will "network out" and become fishers of men.

As soon as the Samaritan woman encounters Jesus, she becomes a missionary to her own village. She abandons her original purpose of fetching water. Leaving her jar at the well she runs to tell her people of her discovery. Her desire to share her experience is all the more remarkable in that she doesn't even seem to be sure yet that Jesus is the Messiah. Yet her question, "Could he be the Messiah?" is enough to draw a crowd of the townsfolk.

Seeing them coming, Jesus reflects on the harvest. Whereas in the Synoptics he says, "The harvest is great, the laborers are few. Pray the Lord of the harvest to send laborers into the harvest" (Mt 9:37-38), in John it seems to be the risen Jesus addressing his disciples entering the Samaritan mission. They are sent as reapers of the work of other sowers (Jesus himself and the woman and perhaps others). The disciples encounter the faith already planted, and the missionaries and the faithful Samaritans rejoice together at the harvest. The networking principle has been effective again. An "unofficial" evangelist, a woman, has evangelized her people ahead of those we might expect to have done the evangelizing. Were the disciples so interested in buying food that they failed to evangelize the shopkeepers from whom they bought it, while Jesus, hungry and thirsty, evangelized the woman who in turn evangelized the town untouched by the disciples? And is Jesus' desire to evangelize as the Father wills, the food that nourishes him more than the food the disciples have brought? ("I have food to eat of which you do not know," 4:32). The lesson for the reader is this: one need not be officially commissioned by Jesus (or the bishop or the parish priest) to share one's faith. Just do it, and it will nourish your spirit better than food nourishes your body.

There is the additional note that once the Samaritans meet Jesus in person they come to believe in him no longer on the basis of the woman's testimony but because of their own personal encounter. Another important lesson: ultimately the people we evangelize must meet not us but Jesus. They must have their personal encounter with the Lord. Job's "hearsay" faith was insufficient to get him through his suffering. Only a personal encounter with the Lord enabled him to say, "Now that my own eye has seen you, I repent in dust and ashes" (Jb 52:3-4). Piggyback faith may work for a while, but it is only a start. We all began that way because the human condition calls for faith to be handed on from one person to another (1 Cor 15:3). But eventually we have to learn to walk for ourselves. Now it is our turn to bring others to Jesus. We offer our shoulders for them to ride on. John the Baptist sets the example: "The one who has the bride is the bridegroom; the best man, who stands and listens for him, rejoices greatly at the bridegroom's voice. So this joy of mine has been made complete. He must increase; I must decrease" (3:29-30).

The networking pattern appears again when the Greek proselytes tell Philip they want to see Jesus (12:20-22). Philip leads them to Andrew (the first "networking" disciple named in 1:40), who in turn leads them to Jesus. This, incidentally, is a significant moment because for Jesus it signals that his hour has come (12:23), and he speaks of the seed that must fall into the ground and die if it is to bear much fruit (12:24). When the Greeks, symbolic of the Gentile world, come upon the stage, the beneficiaries of Jesus' mission are now in place, Gentile alongside Jew, and Jesus can proceed to his saving death for all (3:16).

After Jesus' resurrection, which is his glorification, the same networking pattern continues. Mary Magdalene, the first to meet the risen Lord, announces the news to the disciples (20:18). The disciples tell Thomas, who does not believe until he personally sees Jesus and touches his wounds (20:24-39). This last scene is intentionally addressed to the reader, who should join the network of believers on the basis of the apostolic witness and not because they have physically seen the risen Lord. The glory of Jesus does not, perhaps, shine through the evangelizing disciples as clearly as it did in Jesus, but the same blessing, even a greater one, is as available to those who believe as to those who have seen. Believing is a form of seeing Jesus — equivalent, if not better, than physical sight.

In John, then, evangelizing action is a process of sharing one's personal experience of Jesus with others. The Beloved Disciple, whose testimony is contained in the Gospel (21:24), is a prime example of this sharing, for the Gospel itself is the sharing of his experience of Jesus, as an invitation to believe (20:30-31).

Typical of the Fourth Gospel, the emphasis is upon *personal* interaction and sharing. But that is not the whole story. At the Last Supper Jesus repeatedly stresses mutual love and unity (14:34-35; 15:12-17), especially in his prayer to the Father (chapter 17). And there, in a climax of his teaching, he prays that his disciples will be so united in him with the Father and with each other that "the world may believe that you have sent me" (17:21). The disciples are not to be "Lone Rangers." If God's plan is to gather into one all the dispersed children of God (11:51), then disunity among the gatherers would be a self-defeating sign. Their unity, on the other hand, would be proof positive that God's plan of unity is realizable. The world to be evangelized would have in the disciples a model of what it could become and a powerful invitation to do so. The ultimate source, model, and goal of evangelization and mission in the Church is the inter-personal unity of the Trinity!

This unity is clearly not of human fashioning, though it may take heroic effort to achieve it. It is a gift for which Jesus prays.

Jesus also empowers the disciples to forgive or retain sins (20:22-23), but this appears to be a function of pastoring the flock rather than of personal evangelization. Similarly, Jesus' threefold commission of Peter (21:15-19) is a commissioning to shepherd the flock already constituted. It is, of course, a critical service to the Church, one in which other members may participate in some subordinate way.

John's approach to evangelization is hence very personal, as if almost exclusively one-on-one. Elsewhere in the New Testament we see team ministry, e.g., Paul with Barnabas (Ac 13:2), Paul with Timothy (2 Cor 1:1; Ph 1:1), Paul with Timothy and Silvanus (1 Th 1:1). We also find the attraction of the praying community upon outsiders (1 Cor 14:23-25), preaching (Ac 2:14, 41), and witnessing (Ac 1:8; Rv 1:9) as methods of evangelization. Surely these methods were known and practiced in John's community. But the Beloved Disciple is so overwhelmed by his experience of Jesus' personal love for him that he gives *personal* sharing of that experience pride of place. In so doing he sees evangelization as the earthly extension of the super-abundant life of the Trinity.

Questions for Reflection/Sharing

1. Think of an example from your own life where someone shared their faith with you in a way that led you to a deeper encounter with Jesus.
2. Can you recall a situation where you brought someone to Jesus?
3. Recall an incident in which you were deeply moved by the love and unity of a group. How did it reveal Jesus to you?
4. What grace do you feel called to pray for after reading this chapter?